SOCIETY FOR
HUMAN
RESOURCE
MANAGEMENT

EFFECTIVE HUMAN RESOURCE MEASUREMENT TECHNIQUES

A Handbook for Practitioners

SECOND EDITION

Marc G. Singer
Maureen J. Fleming
Editors

Written and edited primarily by members of the
Society for Human Resource Management
Research Committee

SHRM FOUNDATION
SOCIETY FOR HUMAN RESOURCE MANAGEMENT

This book is published by the Society for Human Resource Management (SHRM) and was funded by a grant from the SHRM Foundation. The interpretations, conclusions, and recommendations, however, are those of the authors and do not necessarily represent those of the Foundation or of SHRM.

ISBN 0-939900-53-x

PREFACE

To promote an understanding of the issues involved in the proper collection, analysis, and use of data, SHRM's national research committee is providing our colleagues with this guide. Written primarily by members of the committee, the text is not meant to be an all-inclusive treatise on any subject. Rather, each author has attempted to provide sufficient materials to enable HR professionals to understand the fundamental concepts of a particular topic. For those of our colleagues who wish to pursue a topic in greater detail, we offer references and suggested readings at the conclusion of each chapter.

The mission of the research committee is to foster the use of applied research and to identify ways to make the use of data easier. Our primary goal in preparing this second edition of *Effective Human Resource Measurement Techniques* was to make it user-friendly. We hope that we have done so. To this end, the research committee welcomes queries on research matters and will try to give assistance whenever possible.

We thank the members of the research committee and the invited authors for their time and efforts in writing and editing this text. We are especially grateful to the SHRM Foundation for funding the project in recognition of the important role of research to the profession. Marlene Nesary, Editorial Director for the University of Montana Bureau of Business and Economic Research, did all of the initial organizing and the first editing work on the book. Finally, we would be remiss in not thanking the professional editorial staff who chopped, sliced, and repaired our work, and the personnel at SHRM, particularly Deborah Keary, who masterfully coordinated the final project.

Marc G. Singer, PhD   Lynda L. Brown, PhD SPHR
Maureen J. Fleming, PhD   Chair, SHRM Research Committee
Editors

ABOUT THE AUTHORS

Ramona B. Akin, EdD, PHR

Ramona B. Akin is professor of business at Henderson State University in Arkadelphia, Arkansas. She received her BSE in 1968 and an MSE in 1972 from Henderson State University, and an EdD in 1975 from the University of Arkansas. Dr. Akin concentrates in the area of employee relations, and her research efforts in the area of sexual harassment have been presented at both national and international conferences. She has been instrumental in the implementation of Quality Teaching Circles at her institution and serves on the SBA Regional Advisory Council. Dr. Akin has previously published in the *Intan Management Journal Malaysia*, and the *International Academy of Case Studies Journal*.

Lynda L. Brown, PhD, SPHR

Lynda L. Brown is director of human resources for St. Patrick Hospital in Missoula, Montana. She received her BS in 1970 from the College of William and Mary, an MEd in 1971 from the University of Oklahoma, and a PhD in 1973 from Florida State University. Dr. Brown has worked as an HR professional in health care and conservation, served as a training and development consultant to organizations, and been a visiting faculty member at Washington State University and the University of Montana. She currently serves as chairperson of SHRM's national research committee and as a member of the SHRM Foundation Board.

Bob Fisher, PhD

Bob Fisher is vice president for academic affairs at Arkansas State University. He received his BSBA in 1970 from Henderson State University, an MBA in 1971 from the University of Memphis, and a PhD in 1975 from the University of Arkansas. A recent Fulbright Scholar to Malaysia, Dr. Fisher is a member of SHRM's national research committee and has served as president of the Arkansas

SHRM chapter. An expert in the areas of testing, organizational development, and work teams, Dr. Fisher is the co-author of a 1996 book titled *Real Dream Teams*.

Maureen J. Fleming, PhD

Maureen J. Fleming is professor of management at the University of Montana. She received her AB in 1963 from Mundelein College, along with a master's in 1966 and a PhD in 1969 from Southern Illinois University. An active member of the Big Sky chapter of SHRM, Dr. Fleming has been involved in SHRM and its predecessor, ASPA, for more than twenty years. An international consultant, Dr. Fleming is a member of SHRM's national research committee, the Academy of Management, the Academy of International Business, the Association of Global Business, the Association of Marketing Theory and Practice, and the International Association of Business Disciplines. She serves as a trustee for the Montana Board of Investments. In addition, she is the current proceedings editor and book editor for the *Journal of Global Business*. Dr. Fleming is widely published in the journals of the organizations in which she has memberships.

H. W. Hennessey, Jr., PhD, SPHR

Harry W. Hennessey, Jr., is professor of management and chair of the Division of Business and Economics at the University of Hawaii in Hilo. He received his BBA in 1972 from Florida Atlantic University, an MA in Counseling in 1976 from the University of North Florida, and a PhD in 1980 from the University of Georgia. Dr. Hennessey is a well-published author whose primary expertise lies in the areas of selection and testing. Most recently, his research interests have centered on the effects of subtle biases in human resource decision-making processes and on certification testing. In addition to serving on SHRM's national research committee, Dr. Hennessey has been actively involved in the Human Resource Certification Institute (HRCI) as a board member, as the national director of examination development, and as the 1996 president.

Before founding ARM, Ms. Swist was a regional consulting manager with McGladrey & Pullen, and manager of the management consulting division of the management association of Illinois (formerly MIMA). In addition to her background as a consultant and practice in corporate HR, Ms. Swist teaches as an adjunct faculty member at National Louis University. Her principal area of expertise and research focus is in organization development, and she was recently published in *Transportation and Distribution Magazine*. Ms. Swist is a member of SHRM's national research committee.

Raymond B. Weinberg, SPHR, CCP

Raymond B. Weinberg is a senior project consultant for Silverstone Consulting, Inc. He received his BSBA in 1973 and his MBA in 1977 from the University of Nebraska at Omaha. Before his current assignment, Mr. Weinberg was director of human resources at Father Flanagan's Boys Home, where he was directly responsible for administering all phases of HR for a 1,700-employee youth care organization operating in 17 cities and 11 states. In addition to his workplace experience, Mr. Weinberg has taught HR-related courses for the past 20 years at several colleges and universities, including Buena Vista University, Metropolitan Community College, and the University of Nebraska at Omaha. Mr. Weinberg is an active member of many professional associations, a member of SHRM's national research committee, and a past president of HRCI. In recognition of his expertise in, and contribution to, the field of HR, Mr. Weinberg was presented with SHRM's prestigious "Award for Professional Excellence" in 1993.

Carolyn Wiley, PhD, SPHR

Carolyn Wiley is UC Foundation associate professor of management at the University of Tennessee at Chattanooga. She received her BS in 1972 and her MA in 1974 from Texas Woman's University, and her PhD in 1982 from the University of California, Los Angeles (UCLA). A much-published author, Dr. Wiley focuses her research and writing endeavors on the areas of staffing, professionalism and certification, compensation, and ethics. Dr. Wiley serves on SHRM's national research committee and as the national membership committee of the Academy of Management. She has been recognized for her scholarship, teaching, and service by being awarded the Summerfield-Johnson Centennial Scholar Award and a UC Foundation Professorship Award from the University of Tennessee at Chattanooga. In 1995, Dr. Wiley was profiled as "an exemplary HR researcher" in the textbook *Human Resource Management* by Megginson, Franklin & Byrd.

CONTENTS

Figures

Tables

CHAPTER 1

RESEARCH METHODOLOGY:
RESEARCH DESIGN AND DATA COLLECTION

Robert W. Hollmann

The quality of human resource (HR) research is affected significantly by its design and methodology. Inappropriate research design and techniques can seriously hamper the reliability and validity of a study and can minimize the study's overall usefulness.

An HR researcher seeking answers to questions or solutions to problems can use a variety of research methodologies. The methods selected will depend on a number of factors such as type and seriousness of the problem, time and staff available, skills of the researcher, and costs. In addition, research methods can vary with respect to complexity, speed, accuracy, and certainty of results or conclusions. This chapter describes some of the more common types of research, basic research designs, and data collection techniques.

Types of Research

There are numerous frameworks for classifying the different research methodologies available to those investigating HR issues. One framework considers research as pure, basic, or applied. Most HR research is *applied research*, which consists of examining specific situations in hopes of providing practical solutions.

Quantitative research uses methodologies that collect, analyze, and interpret quantitative data. *Qualitative research* relies on the use of nonquantitative information and analysis, and it usually involves such activities as reporting, describing, and subjectively interpreting.

Primary research consists of studies performed directly by the researcher through such methodologies as case studies, organizational surveys, and field experiments. *Secondary research* is conducted by other persons or organizations and is reported in a variety of published documents.

Research Design

Selecting the overall design of a research study is a function of the objective of the study, the specific problem to be examined, and the hypotheses to be tested.

Historical Studies. This design involves a retrospective analysis of past activities and events through the review of organizational documents, records, data, and testimony of participants and observers. On the one hand, the approach is limited by the fact that the researcher must use opinion, interpretation, and judgment about the validity and reliability of information collected. On the other hand, a longitudinal analysis often can provide the researcher with meaningful insights into behavior and activities within an organization. The key to this approach is to isolate a few main factors or variables for examination and then to use organizational data to track them over time.

Many of the topics discussed in this handbook (e.g., absenteeism, turnover, employee satisfaction, etc.) can be examined through a historical study. For example, a 2-year historical study of absenteeism data may provide some preliminary insights into the effectiveness of a newly implemented absenteeism control program.

It is also possible that the results of a historical study can serve as the basis of a hypothesis for a more rigorous research design such as a controlled experiment. For instance, a review of longitudinal data about employee satisfaction may suggest that alternative scheduling of work has resulted in higher satisfaction and productivity. Then a controlled experiment could be conducted to see if a causal relationship does in fact exist.

Case Studies. A case study consists of in-depth data gathering, observation, and analysis of the wide range of circumstances associated with a single event or situation. Case study data are obtainable through documents, interviews, and observations.

Because a case study focuses on a particular situation, its results cannot be generalized to other situations. However, the findings of a case study often serve as the foundation for additional analyses. Sometimes a series of similar cases suggests specific hypotheses for testing in a more rigorous study. For example, a researcher may perform a case study of an organization's efforts to introduce microcomputers into a particular phase of its operations. The results of this study could form a basis to examine a number of different change efforts throughout the organization. The final product of these studies might be a series of guidelines for managers to follow when introducing technology-based changes.

Surveys. A considerable amount of organizational research is conducted through a survey research design, which can involve either a polling survey or an analytical survey. A *polling survey* is used to examine current practices and techniques. The results are descriptive and are useful in making intraorganizational or interorganizational comparisons. The survey can be replicated at different times and in different organizational units. Most surveys of employee attitude or morale are polling surveys.

An *analytical survey* takes the data collected in a polling survey and subjects it to statistical analysis. Distinctions are made between data groups, and various statistical tests are applied to ascertain if there are differences or relationships between the groups. An example is an organization-wide morale survey in which the data are gathered and divided into various employee and morale factor groupings; then statistical analyses, such as correlations and difference testing, are performed among the groups. However, establishing correlations between groups of data does not indicate a cause-and-effect relationship nor does it indicate if the same relationship will exist under different circumstances.

Experiments. Experiments represent the most rigorous form of human resource research. The previously described techniques do not allow the researcher to draw any conclusions regarding *causality*. For example, consider the case where an organization sends its first-level supervisors to a leadership training program, and a 2-year historical study later shows significant reductions in absenteeism and turnover. The historical study design does not allow the researcher to conclude with any degree of certainty that the improvement in absenteeism and turnover was due to the training received by those supervisors. Perhaps it was due to a new compensation plan or improvements in the employee benefit program.

To make any conclusions about causality, researchers should use a controlled experiment. This approach "controls" for or weeds out other possible explanations of the changes that have occurred. While a detailed description of experimental design is beyond the scope of this chapter, some basic guidelines relative to the establishment of such experiments will be offered. Readers interested in greater detail are referred to the work of Cook and Campbell (1979).

Basically, an experimental design requires that at least two groups be used. One group is exposed to the "treatment" that is being studied and is known as the *experimental group*. The other group is not exposed to the treatment and is known as the *control group*. Measures are taken for both groups before (pre-test) and after (post-test) the treatment and then these measures are compared. If there is a change for the experimental group but not for the control group, then it is suggested that the change occurred because of the treatment.

An example of this design might be an organization evaluating the effectiveness of a training program. In the scenario described in the previous paragraph, the "treatment" is the actual training program. The pre-test and post-test measures gauge the extent to which employees can perform whatever they are supposed to learn in the training program. The experimental group is the group of employees who went through the training program and the control group is an equivalent group of employees who did not go through the training program.

Additional rigor can be achieved within the experimental design by assigning employees to the experimental and control groups on a random basis. Each group should be large enough to prevent chance characteristics from occurring within it because those chance characteristics might influence relationships found between the groups.

Data Collection Techniques

The HR researcher can collect data through a wide range of techniques. Once again, the techniques used should be a function of the research objective and the research design. This section describes some of the more common data collection techniques.

Questionnaires. The most common method of data collection for a survey research design is the questionnaire, which allows the researcher to obtain information from a large number of respondents in a relatively short time. For example, an employee morale survey is a typical way to assess the attitudes of a large number of employees toward a number of factors that might impact their productivity. Using anonymous questionnaires increases the likelihood of their being returned. Well-designed questionnaire surveys can be an extremely useful way to collect data on a wide range of HR matters.

Interviews. Meaningful research data alsocan be gathered through face-to-face interviews with employees. The interview format can be "structured" or "nonstructured." In the former case, the interviewer has a specific set of questions that are asked of all interviewees (e.g., "Were you able to work effectively with co-employees under the flextime approach and, if not, what specific problems did you encounter?") In the nonstructured approach, the interviewer asks open-ended questions (e.g., "What do you think of flextime program?") The structured approach is recommended because it results in greater clarity, reliability, and validity of answers. A major advantage of the interview method is that the interviewer has the chance to ask for additional explanation.

Literature Reviews. A considerable amount of HR research is published in a wide variety of professional and scholarly journals. It is instructive for a HR researcher to review relevant literature before embarking on a planned study. The literature may show results of similar efforts, and it may alert the researcher to possible study results and possible problems in performing the study. Figure 1–1 lists relevant journals. Computer software now is available that makes literature searches much easier. The SHRM Information Center and Library also is an excellent resource.

External Surveys. It is not unusual for external organizations to conduct local, regional, or national surveys on HR issues. Before starting a research project, the researcher may wish to review surveys already conducted by such organizations as the Bureau of National Affairs, the Commerce Clearing House, and the U.S. Bureau of Labor Statistics.

Third-Party Studies. Research conducted by third parties can provide the researcher with helpful data and information. SHRM has supported specific research studies and made the results available to its membership. SHRM headquarters or the SHRM Foundation may have relevant results available. Other sources of research include private consulting firms and the faculty at local colleges and universities.

The Importance of Reliability and Validity

For HR research to be meaningful and useful, studies must have high levels of reliability and validity. One can have little confidence in results obtained through unreliable instruments or through research designs and instruments with low validity. Readers are referred to chapter 4, "Understanding Job Analysis, Validity, and Reliability in Selection," for a more thorough discussion of reliability and validity.

Human Resource Information Systems

The quality of HR research is affected not only by study design and data collection methods but also by the actual data used. These data must be accurate and timely. For example, research on the potential adverse impact of employment practices may be extremely difficult without a whole range of data, such as organizational workforce characteristics and labor market statistics.

Figure 1–1. Professional Journals

Academy of Management Journal

Administrative Science Quarterly

American Journal of Sociology

American Psychologist

Behavioral Science

Decision Sciences

HRMagazine (formerly *Personnel Administrator*)

Human Resource Management

Industrial and Labor Relations Review

Industrial Relations

Journal of Applied Behavioral Science

Journal of Applied Psychology

Journal of Business Research

Journal of International Business Studies

Journal of Management Studies

Journal of Social Psychology

Monthly Labor Review

Organizational Behavior and Human Decision Processes (formerly *Organizational Behavior and Human Performance*)

Personnel

Personnel Administrator

Personnel Journal

Personnel Psychology

Public Personnel Management

Social Science Research

Selection of a research design is contingent on the availability of quality data. The importance of quality data normally requires that the HR researcher collaborate with human resource information system (HRIS) employees. These employees usually understand the nature and the details of data in organizational computer files, and they should be involved in the early stages of research design. HRIS specialists can offer a great deal of help to the HR researcher in obtaining and analyzing data via the latest computer technology, including such sources as the Internet.

References and Suggested Readings

Bateman, T. S., & Ferris, G. R. (Eds.). (1984). *Methods and analysis in organizational research.* Reston, VA: Reston Publishing.

Cook, J. D., & Campbell, D. T. (1979). *Quasi-experimental design and analysis for field settings.* Chicago: Rand-McNally.

Hollmann, R. W. (1994). HRM/D research. In W. R. Tracey, *Human resources management & development handbook* (2nd ed., pp. 381–396). New York: AMACOM (American Management Association).

Schmitt, N. W., & Klimoski, R. J. (1991). *Research methods in human resources management.* Cincinnati, OH: South-Western Publishing.

CHAPTER 2

ETHICAL RESEARCH

Ellen R. Singer

HR practitioners, by the very nature of their work, are inherently researchers. They employ research informally and systematically to understand, manage, and enrich the environments of employees and organizations. Major human research functions such as strategic planning, job analysis, job evaluation, selection and placement, performance appraisal, and training involve the use of analytical skills. Efforts directed at assessing HR effectiveness, such as HR audits, also fall within the domain of HR research. An operative knowledge of research techniques allows HR personnel to ask intelligent questions, to aggregate and analyze data appropriately, to make informed decisions, to solve problems, and to plan for future contingencies. In other words, "research on personnel management activities provides an understanding of what works, what does not work, and what needs to be done" (Mathis & Jackson, 1985, p. 527).

In the course of conducting organizational research, HR practitioners encounter a variety of ethical issues. Practical research generally occurs in natural settings, where researchers have less control over individuals and circumstances. Therefore, conflicts among scientific principles; real working conditions; and multiple values, conflicting values, or both are virtually inevitable. Unfortunately, during the research process, ethical matters are sometimes slighted, compromised, or overshadowed by other considerations. However, it is important to note that the use of unprincipled means in the execution of research is justified neither by the scientific ends nor the esoteric purposes of a particular inquiry. Although thoughtfully designed research methodology furnishes individuals and organizations with useful information, it must be ethically as well as methodologically sound to be worthwhile.

Informed and Voluntary Consent

The principle of informed consent requires researchers to apprise potential participants about a study before their involvement in it. Furthermore, participants should be advised that they have the right to withdraw their consent at any time during the research process. Since organizational research frequently takes place in the field, it is especially important for individuals to understand that a decision to enlist, to decline, or to withdraw from a research project will not affect their job outcomes. Although informed consent cannot always be obtained, researchers should routinely pursue this ideal. Employing this practice respects and protects the rights of individuals by affording them autonomy and the opportunity to make discerning choices concerning participation.

Informed and voluntary consent may be obtained in various ways. For example, when conducting survey research, a short introduction explaining the nature and purpose of the research should be included in the survey. Consent of potential participants is confirmed or denied by whether or not they complete the survey. The introduction should also assure participants that their responses will be kept confidential and separate from other personnel information. Figure 2–1 illustrates a sample questionnaire introduction.

Figure 2–1. Sample Questionnaire Introduction

Dear Employee,

The HR department is conducting research about employee attitudes toward a new scheduling policy. The purpose of this questionnaire is to give you an opportunity to tell how you feel about this policy. Please try to answer every question. Your answers to all of the questions will be coded anonymously, and they will in no way have anything to do with how your work performance is evaluated.

Thank you for your cooperation.

Figure 2–2 is an example of a consent form that could be used to secure an individual's permission to be interviewed for a research project. Under these circumstances, the interviewer should code all interview notes so that they cannot be connected to the interviewee at a later time. Note that in this format the participant's signed permission is requested.

Figure 2–2. Sample Consent Form

You are invited to participate in a research study that is conducted by the HR department and explores how employees feel about a new scheduling policy. You will be asked questions about the current and the new policies. Your participation in this study will involve an interview of approximately 30 minutes and will be audiotaped.

Please understand that your participation in this study is voluntary. You have the right to refuse to answer particular questions, or you may withdraw your consent or discontinue participation at any time without penalty. In addition, your individual privacy will be maintained in all published and written materials resulting from this study. The information will not be shared with any of your supervisors or managers and will have nothing to do with how your work performance is evaluated.

Thank you for your cooperation.

Signed _____

Date _____

Privacy Issues

It is self-evident that falsification and misrepresentation of data breach the ethical code of research conduct. A related ethical challenge involves ensuring the privacy of employees, clients, or organizations engaged in the research process. "The right to privacy may be looked upon as the right of the individual to decide the extent to which attitudes, opinions, behaviors, and personal facts will be shared with others" (Stone, 1978, p. 147). Since information obtained during the research process is confidential, ethical practices oblige investigators to treat research data and outcomes judiciously and confidentially. However, the confidentiality ethic does not extend to study participants who have a prior understanding that the results will be shared with others. With the participant's consent, the researcher may ethically disclose information to others or use the information in supplemental formats such as reports or presentations.

Specific research procedures are available to safeguard the anonymity and confidentiality of individuals and institutions. Ideally, questionnaires should be designed so that participants may respond anonymously, eliminating the need to code the responses. However, if complete anonymity cannot be realized, questionnaires may be coded blindly so that it is not feasible for specific institutions or respondents to be connected to the data. Gathering data in this manner not only secures the privacy of the survey participants but also increases the probability that individuals will be willing to participate in the study. Furthermore, respondents are more likely to provide truthful responses, especially to sensitive questions. Since blind coding enhances the accuracy of the data collected, this method serves a functional as well as an ethical purpose for HR professionals.

Ensuring privacy applies not only to planned research activities but also to the daily HR enterprise. For example, decisions concerning the acquisition and dissemination of information in employee records are ethical dilemmas that frequently confront HR personnel. Since state laws and company policies vary in relation to the accessibility and use of information in personnel records, ethical concerns can be heightened. Sometimes, complete anonymity is infeasible. In circumstances where private information is inappropriately managed or carelessly handled, the potential for unethical behavior escalates.

Ethical dilemmas may be minimized by organizational policies that facilitate employee confidentiality. For example, an HR protocol may be initiated to restrict the access of employee records to appropriate personnel and on a need basis only. This protocol, monitored by a "guardian of the records," might include the following information: the names of the individuals requesting and releasing the record, the date of the record's release and return, and the purpose of request. A specified time period for record retention may be included as well. A supplemental and favorable outcome of this red tape is that it may discourage individuals from making unnecessary requests for records.

There are additional practices that would further promote the ethic of employee confidentiality. These methods address both research and more practical perspectives. The procedures include the following:

- Interpreting research findings and other data concerning employees objectively rather than subjectively;

- Reporting research findings in general rather than specific terms;

- Destroying research data or other employee information that are no longer necessary or legally required;

- Keeping records separate (i.e., medical and performance review);

- Divulging only necessary information, rather than complete files; and

- Training personnel to treat employee information prudently.

Resolving Ethical Dilemmas

Because ethical dilemmas are inevitable realities of organizational research, HR professionals should be highly sensitive to their personal, academic, practical, and legal implications. Ethical dilemmas are difficult to resolve because individuals and circumstances are often complex, variable, and ambiguous. In instances where ethical issues must be settled singularly, decision making becomes even more burdensome. Reconciling ethical dilemmas may be facilitated to some degree by consulting laws, codes of research ethics, and internal or external research committees. Sharing and rotating ethical decision making responsibilities among HR personnel whenever feasible are also beneficial practices. These approaches not only expand the accountability for decision making but also minimize the stress frequently associated with making ethical choices.

Although the legal system is open to interpretation and revision, it still offers HR personnel a concrete framework to guide some of their decision making during the research process. For example, questions about what makes an employment test valid, or why a selection technique is discriminatory may be settled in a court of law. However, when ethical decisions do not have the benefit of legal parameters or precedents, they are more difficult to reconcile. Confronted by equivocal guidelines and obscure issues, individuals frequently make decisions based on personal standards. This strategy may cause attitudinal, behavioral, and role inconsistencies because of variations across individuals' value systems (Mirvis & Seashore, 1979). For example, the use of deception in a research study is viewed by some methodologists as legitimate in certain circumstances and deemed unethical by others under any conditions (Stone, 1978).

Academicians and other professionals (i.e., attorneys and psychologists) can provide valuable resources to HR professionals engaged in research. For example, a human subjects research committee from a nearby college or university can be engaged to review a proposed project or to answer specific questions concerning research methodology. The HR department may also form its own ethics committee to explore the ramifications of various research methods and procedures. Finally, codes of research ethics may be consulted for answers to questions about a variety of ethical principles and practices. Numerous organizations, among them the American Psychological Association (1981a, 1981b), have issued such codes.

Research contributes significantly to the theory and practice of human resource management. A functional body of research knowledge provides HR professionals with scientific paradigms to interpret real world phenomena and to solve real world problems by engaging in more than trial-and-error-based solutions. However, the process of HR research also creates an exacting enterprise fraught with difficult questions and conflicting methods. The professional response to this challenge must acknowledge from the onset that the difficulties inherent in HR research, realistic as they may be, cannot be cited to rationalize unethical or slipshod research practices. For HR inquiry to be meaningful and practical, it must embrace a human and a scientific ethic.

References and Suggested Readings

Adair, J. G. (1988). Research on research ethics. *American Psychologist, 43*(10), 825–826.

American Psychological Association. (1974). *Standards for educational and psychological tests.* Washington, DC: Author.

American Psychological Association. (1981a). Ethical principles of psychologists. *American Psychologist, 36*(6), 633–638.

American Psychological Association. (1981b). Specialty guidelines for the delivery of services by industrial/organizational psychologists. *American Psychologist, 36*(6), 664–669.

Blanck, P. D., Bellack, A. S., Rosnow, R. L., & Rotheram-Borus, M. J. (1992). Scientific rewards and conflicts of ethical choices in human subjects research. *American Psychologist, 47*(7), 959–965.

Caplan, A. L., & Callahan, D. (Eds.). (1981). *Ethics in hard times.* Hastings-on-the-Hudson, NY: The Hastings Center, Institute of Society, Ethics, and the Life Sciences.

Grisso, T., Baldwin, E., Blanck, P. D., & Rotheram-Borus, M. J. (1991). Standards in research: APA's mechanism for monitoring the challenges. *American Psychologist, 46*(7), 758–766.

Kahn, W. A. (1990). Toward an agenda for business ethics research. *Academy of Management Review, 15*(2), 311–328.

London, M., & Bray, D. W. (1980). Ethical issues in testing and evaluation for personnel decisions. *American Psychologist, 35*(10), 890–901.

Lowman, R. (1985). *Casebook on ethics and standards for the practice of psychology in organizations.* College Park, MD: Society for Industrial and Organizational Psychology.

Mathis, R. L., & Jackson, J. H. (1985). *Personnel human resource management* (4th ed.). St. Paul, MN: West Publishing.

Mirvis, P. H., & Seashore, S. E. (1979). Being ethical in organizational research. *American Psychologist, 34*(9), 766–780.

Randall, D. M., & Gibson, A. M. (1990). Methodology in business ethics research: A review and critical assessment. *Journal of Business Ethics, 9*(6), 457–471.

Schlitz, M. E. (Ed.). (1992). *Standards in institutional research.* San Francisco: Jossey-Bass.

Schrader-Frechette, K. S. (1994). *Ethics of scientific research.* Lanham, MD: Rowman & Littlefield.

Sieber, J. E. (1977). What is meant by ethics? *American Psychologist, 32*(8), 684–685.

Sieber, J. E. (1994). Will the new code help researchers to be more ethical? Special Section: The 1992 ethics codes: Boon or bane? *Professional Psychology Research and Practice, 25*(4), 369–375.

Stone, E. F. (1978). *Research methods in organizational behavior.* Santa Monica, CA: Goodyear Publishing.

CHAPTER 3

PRE-EMPLOYMENT TESTING

Ramona B. Akin and Bob Fisher

Many companies try to improve their employee selection process through a variety of approaches to pre-employment testing. This testing can decrease hiring costs and reduce the number of employee terminations.

Testing is used to predict employee tenure as well as other aspects of the employment situation such as customer relations, work values, and safety. Psychologists can identify candidates who are likely to leave an organization by exploring their intentions to quit, their anticipated job satisfaction, their beliefs about normal behavior among workers, and their beliefs about the best way to advance their own careers. Testing can provide information about technical capabilities for certain jobs, as well as the ability to learn.

Pre-employment tests vary from industry to industry, depending on which factors are being measured.

Screening and Work Sample Tests

A work sample test requires an applicant to actually perform a sample of the work that will be done on the job. This test is performed in a controlled situation and replicates actual job requirements. For example, an applicant for a clerical position might be given a typing test. A psychomotor or finger dexterity test could be used for a job that requires the ability to work with small items; a space visualization test could be used for an applicant under consideration for a draftsperson's position.

The purpose of these tests is to screen out candidates who are obviously unqualified.

Aptitude Tests

An aptitude test, in contrast, is designed to measure an applicant's general ability to learn or acquire a skill. To illustrate, an employer might use the Wonderlic Personnel Test, the Hay Number Perception Test, and the Hay Name Finding Test in combination to determine whether a prospective employee would be able to learn quickly and whether that individual would be fast and accurate with both number- and word-oriented tasks.

Honesty Tests

Honesty tests are typically used by companies to detect prospective employees who are at high risk for dishonest behaviors. These tests are intended to measure honesty, integrity, counterproductivity, employee deviance, wayward impulses, organizational delinquency, absenteeism, dependability, emotional stability, job performance, predictability, service orientation, and stress tolerance.

Typical paper-and-pencil honesty tests include two types of items. While the first group of items asks test-takers about past behaviors regarding theft or impropriety, the second group of items inquires about their attitudes toward theft or impropriety. These tests are aimed at identifying individuals an employer would want to hire—those who would not be detrimental to the organization.

Graphoanalysis

Somewhat related to the honesty test is graphoanalysis, or the analysis of handwriting. Graphoanalysis uses handwriting analysis to identify personality characteristics and suitability for employment. The use of this controversial method of analysis has grown since the Employee Polygraph Protection Act of 1988 made it illegal for most private organizations to use the polygraph as a selection device.

Drug Tests

Many employers advocate drug testing because of its advantages in the areas of reduced health care coverage costs and increased productivity. Where not prohibited by law, drug tests can be administered to all applicants and current employees.

While drug testing may reduce the applicant pool, it can help organizations attract a higher caliber of employee, ensure a safer workplace, and facilitate delivery of better quality products and service. Drug testing is also helpful in the fight against substance abuse.

Impairment Testing

Because of some resistance to drug testing on the basis that it may be considered a violation of the right to privacy, some organizations are now using impairment testing instead. This type of test is designed to detect actual impairment of motor skills and hand-eye coordination rather than the chemical "metabolite" that the drug test detects. The computer used for this test cannot be fooled because it reacts to the individual's performance. However, impairment testing requires baseline data for comparison purposes. Thus, it would be more appropriately used during a probationary period than as an actual pre-employment test.

Assessment Centers

In assessment centers, candidates are observed in simulated work situations. These candidates perform certain parts of the job for which they are being considered and are evaluated on their ability to make decisions, handle conflict, set priorities, and communicate.

The process generally requires 1 to 3 days and may cost an additional $750 to $1,000 per hire, depending on how many applicants are involved.

The in-basket or in-box exercise is a behavioral test that is usually included in assessment center evaluation. The in-basket is designed to provide feedback about a candidate's time management, organization, and decision-making skills. Interaction simulations, panel interviews, mock staff meetings, and other work simulations involving several employees are also included.

Speeded vs. Power Tests

Several of the tests previously described can be in the form of either a speeded test or a power test. A speeded test, in its utmost simplicity, consists of very elementary and similar items. Perfect scores would be anticipated from most examinees if they were given sufficient time. However, strict time limitations are dictated so that the test measures processing speed.

A power test measures a person's expertise in a given subject area without concern for how quickly the items are answered. A pure power test would be administered without time limits. However, a power test can be subjected to realistic time limitations. Two well-known academic examples of these timed power tests include the Graduate Record Exam and the Scholastic Achievement Test.

Sources for Test Information

Information about various tests can be found in the *Mental Measurement Yearbooks* (*MMY*), *Tests in Print* (*TIP*), and through the Educational Testing Service (ETS).

MMY and *TIP* are both publications of the Buros Institute of Mental Measurement, 135 Bancroft Hall, The University of Nebraska-Lincoln, Lincoln, Nebraska 68588-0348. The Buros Institute also publishes monographs covering specific areas of testing.

The *MMY* provides descriptive information on 418 tests, references, and 803 test reviews. The criteria for inclusion of tests in the *MMY* are that they must be new or revised since the last publication, or they must have generated 20 or more references, plus they must be commercially available and published in English.

The *MMY* contains a bibliography, critical test reviews, a test title index, a classified subject index, a publisher's index and directory, a name index, and a score index. The *MMY* also gives the price of each test listed.

TIP is a descriptive listing and reference without reviews of commercially published tests. The criteria for inclusion in *TIP* are simple. Tests must be in print and available for purchase. *TIP* contains a comprehensive bibliography of tests and references, a test title index, a classified subject index, a publisher's directory, and a name index.

Tests in Print IV (*TIP IV*) provides information on over 4,000 test instruments. The information can assist test users in identifying suitable instruments, evaluating the intent of those instruments, finding relevant reviews, and contacting publishers.

TIP IV can be obtained from the Buros Institute of Mental Measurement. The cost is $325 plus shipping.

The *MMY* and *TIP* are interlocking volumes with extensive cross referencing, and their coordinated use as a system is necessary. *TIP* serves as a comprehensive index to the contents of the *MMY*.

The ETS is an extensive library of 1,500 tests and other measurement devices. ETS was established to provide information on tests and to assess materials for those in research, advisory services, education, and related activities. ETS has a variety of tests designed for particular types of occupations as well as evaluation instruments for assessing certain types of professionals.

Each ETS entry contains test title, author, descriptors, identifiers, availability sources, and an abstract. The publication date, number of test items, and time required to complete the test are also given.

Legal Issues

Pre-employment testing evokes concerns about legal issues in the minds of many HR professionals. The answers to three key questions can help clarify whether a test is likely to withstand legal challenges:

1. Is the test valid? That is, does it measure what it claims to measure, and is the factor being measured an important job-related requirement? For example, testing an applicant's motor dexterity is likely to be considered valid if the position under consideration is in manufacturing assembly. However, a dexterity test would be of limited validity for a position in sales.

2. Is the test reliable? Reliability refers to the stability of test results over time. If one set of results is achieved today and a similar set of results is achieved by repeating the test tomorrow, then the test is likely to be considered reliable.

3. Will the test have an adverse impact on a "protected" group? Existing legislation protects employment opportunities for several groups including women, ethnic minorities, people with disabilities, people in certain age groups, and others. If it can be shown that a particular test results in less desirable scores for the people in these protected groups, then the fairness of the test becomes suspect and employment decisions based on the test are vulnerable to legal challenge.

In today's litigious society, legal counsel should be consulted for advice on decisions that are considered to have the potential for legal challenge.

Conclusion

While an organization may choose to develop its own tests, many predeveloped tests are available from outside sources. It is important that tests be carefully chosen to fit the needs of the organization.

Proper employee selection aided by appropriate pre-employment testing can mean more qualified employees who fit into the organization. The use of suitable selection strategies enhances human resources—the greatest asset that most businesses have.

References and Suggested Readings

Anfuso, D. (1995). Look beyond skills when making hiring decisions. *Personnel Journal, 74*(3), 94.

Assessment centers help target employees for management selection. (1993). *Personnel Journal, 72*(1), 551–552.

Caudron, S. (1994). Team staffing requires new HR role. *Personnel Journal, 73*(5), 88–94.

Fine, C. R. (1992). Video tests are the new frontier in drug detection. *Personnel Journal, 71*(6), 150–161.

Flynn, G. (1994). Attracting the right employees—and keeping them. *Personnel Journal, 73*(12), 44–49.

Flynn, G. (1995). Score A+ employees with pre-employment testing. *Personnel Journal, 74*(8), 6–10.

Forsberg, M. (1992). Custom training on a budget. *Personnel Journal, 71*(4), 112–119.

Lasson, E. D. (1992). How good are integrity tests? *Personnel Journal, 71*(4), 35–37.

Leary, W. E. (1995, April 8). Federal agency rules that using gene tests to deny employment is illegal. *New York Times, p. 7.*

Lilienfeld, S. O. (1993, Fall). Do "honesty" tests really measure honesty? *Skeptical Inquirer, 18*(1), 32–41.

Lipman, I. A. (1996, January). Drug testing is vital in the workplace. *USA Today, 124,* p. 81-82.

Martin, S. L., & Lehnen, L. P. (1992). Select the right employees through testing. *Personnel Journal, 71*(2), 46–51.

McDaniel, L. (1995). Group assessments produce better hires. *HRMagazine, 40*(5), 72–76.

Mead, A. D., & Drasgow, F. (1993). Equivalence of computerized and paper-and-pencil cognitive ability tests: A meta-analysis. *Psychological Bulletin, 114*(3), 449–458.

Segal, J. A. (1992). To test or not to test. *HRMagazine, 37*(4), 40–43.

Sherrid, P. A. (1994). A 12-hour test of my personality. *U.S. News and World Report, 117*(17), 109.

Smith, R. E. (1994, Winter). Corporations that fail the fair hiring test. *Business and Society Review, 88,* 29–33.

Solomon, R. J. (1993). How medical practices can find the right front-office employees through testing. *Personnel Journal, 72*(1), SS4–SS5.

Tennesen, M. (1994). HR faces distinct issues in rural areas. *Personnel Journal, 73*(6), 112–117.

Uhrich, M. D. (1992). Are you positive the test is positive? *HRMagazine, 37*(4), 44–48.

CHAPTER 4

UNDERSTANDING JOB ANALYSIS, VALIDITY, AND RELIABILITY IN SELECTION

Marc G. Singer

The adequate selection and placement of employees have traditionally been two of the most important functions performed by HR managers. Successfully accomplishing these functions requires a great deal of initial planning. Properly conducted selection procedures require that HR managers conduct adequate job analyses, gather statistics regarding the available labor pool, validate instruments, and become familiar with the prevailing legislation governing the selection process. When proper procedures are created, validated, and applied, employees are hired who possess the knowledge, skills, and abilities (KSAs) to satisfactorily perform the jobs in question. Haphazard, hastily conducted approaches may result in workforces that exhibit high turnover and absenteeism, low morale, and poor productivity. Furthermore, if improperly conducted selection methods are found to adversely affect protected group members, costly litigation may follow.

Job Analysis

The goal of any selection process is to assess the KSAs of applicants and compare these KSAs to the job requirements. Applicants whose KSAs show that they can satisfactorily perform the jobs in question are hired. Those candidates whose KSAs do not match the job requirements are rejected. While this process sounds simple enough, it requires initially that a comprehensive job analysis be undertaken and subsequently be validated in order to determine the necessary job requirements. Skipping these processes, or conducting sketchy analyses, may result in a job analysis that misses the essential details necessary to make fine discriminations among candidates. Furthermore, poorly conducted job analyses rarely meet the guidelines for proof of nondiscrimination required by equal employment rules and regulations.

There are several methods for conducting job analyses. Some of these procedures involve obtaining needed information by questioning job incumbents or supervisors via interviews, questionnaires, or both. These methods require the development of questions specifically aimed at the jobs in question. Other techniques, such as Functional Job Analysis (Fine & Wiley, 1973) and the Position Analysis Questionnaire (McCormick, Jeanneret, & Mecham, 1972) provide structure, quantitative procedures, or both for deciding the necessary job requirements. No matter which methods HR managers use, job analyses should be the first step in the selection and validation process.

The Candidate Pool

Sometimes, the necessity for refined selection procedures is negated by the job characteristics and the available labor force. On the one hand, if the job calls for unskilled personnel and is performed under less than desirable working conditions, and if there are few applicants to choose from, the likelihood that sophisticated selection procedures are necessary is small. On the other hand, when jobs are highly skilled, and when there are many more candidates than positions available, HR managers must be more discriminating in their selection techniques. To determine the available labor pool, HR managers calculate the selection ratio.

The selection ratio is obtained by dividing the number of candidates hired by the number of applicants available in the pool, as shown next.

$$\text{Selection Ratio} = \frac{\text{Number of Candidates Hired}}{\text{Number of Candidates Available}}$$

When this ratio is high, it reduces the need for highly selective procedures, while a low ratio requires more complex techniques. Obviously, a low ratio requires more sophisticated selection instruments, and the necessity for validation becomes self-evident.

Validity and Reliability

Any selection instruments used should measure applicant characteristics accurately and consistently. The term *validity* refers to the technique's ability to truly measure what it is supposed to measure, and the term *reliability* means that the technique measures these areas consistently over time.

While the above definition of validity appears to be straightforward, it has occasionally been misunderstood. If a selection technique is valid, this does not necessarily imply that the instrument itself is valid; it means only that the inferences made on the basis of the assessment technique are valid (American Psychological Association, 1974). For example, suppose that an applicant who receives a score of 68 on a skills test is rejected for a job because a score of 70 is required for employment. The reason for the rejection is the assumption that a candidate who scores 70 or above could successfully complete the job requirements, while anybody who scores 69 or below could not. It is not the test itself that is being validated, but rather the candidate's ability to succeed as demonstrated by the test.

While several validation techniques are useful in deciding the merits of measurement instruments, two validation strategies have principally been used by the Equal Employment Opportunity Commission (Gatewood & Schoenfeldt, 1977). These are criterion-related validity (predictive and concurrent) and content validity.

Criterion-related validity statistically examines the relationship between the predictor (measurement instrument) and the criterion (job performance). The difference between the two types of criterion-related validity lies in the timing of when the data for analysis are gathered. Predictive validity requires that the predictor information be gathered early and the criterion data be accumulated over time. Subsequently, the data are compared and the validity is calculated based on the strength of the relationship between the test and success on the job. For example, suppose that an organization has developed a test to determine managerial ability. The test would be administered to position applicants, but since it has not yet been validated, it would not be employed in the selection procedure. Over time, performance evaluation data on the chosen applicants would be accumulated. This information would ultimately be compared statistically with the test data that were collected earlier to decide whether a strong correlation exists.

Unlike predictive validity, which requires administrating a test to new hires and subsequent gathering of performance data, concurrent validity uses existing employees for the validation technique. Thus, the instrument is administered to current employees and results are correlated with their performance data. Again, the instrument's validity as a predictor of ultimate job success would be decided by the strength of the correlation obtained.

Choosing the appropriate validation strategy requires that organizations consider certain factors. On the one hand, predictive validity, requiring the collection of data over time, suffers from several obvious problems. First, when the organization has high turnover, employees are not with the company long enough for the collection of criterion data. Second, when job requirements change rapidly because of factors such as technology, measures developed to ascertain specific job requirements become outdated before validation data can be collected. Finally, small organizations may not have enough candidates for the necessary norm basis to obtain meaningful and significant results.

On the other hand, concurrent validity also has its difficulties. Because it is administered to current employees, the motivation to perform may be minimal. Employees may view the taking of the test as just another bothersome chore. Furthermore, selection measures are designed to indicate which employees will eventually succeed on the job. We can refer to this as the *principle of potentiality*, the ability to succeed in the future on the basis of KSAs and acquired knowledge and training. The scores of current employees may be inflated by knowledge they gleaned on the job and may not reflect how they would have scored as applicants. Thus, rather than an aptitude assessment, the selection technique becomes an achievement measure.

When quantitative measures of validation are inappropriate, content validation is used. Unlike the criterion-related validation strategies, which use statistical measures, content validation relies on the judgment of experts. This technique usually involves three steps. First, a comprehensive job analysis is conducted that identifies the KSAs necessary for job success. Second, the measure for assessing applicant's possession of these KSAs is developed. Finally, the test items are examined by the job incumbents, the experts, to determine whether they adequately sample the job (Arvey, 1988).

Together with validity, HR managers also obtain a measure of reliability or consistency of their measurement tools. To be of value, selection techniques must yield consistent results from administration to administration and from candidate to candidate. The reliability of a measure can be determined through methods such as test-retest reliability and equivalent or parallel forms reliability.

Test-retest reliability is obtained by administering a measure to a group of applicants on one occasion and retesting them later. Obviously, the scores from both administrations should be statistically comparable.

Equivalent or parallel forms reliability requires the development of two comparable instruments that are administered to the same group of individuals. Again, to demonstrate reliability, the scores of both measures should be relatively equal.

Although validity can range from −1 (indicating a perfect negative correlation) to 1, both validity and reliability coefficients are typically reported as numbers between 0 (no validity or reliability) and 1 (perfect validity or reliability). Obviously, the closer to 1, the better. In practice, however, validity coefficients usually range from .30 to .45 (Siegel & Lane, 1987), and reliability coefficients above .70 are usually acceptable (Muchinsky, 1990).

References and Suggested Readings

American Psychological Association. (1974). *Standards for educational and psychological tests.* Washington, DC: Author.

Arvey, R. D. (1988). *Fairness in selecting employees* (2nd ed.). Reading, MA: Addison-Wesley.

Fine, S. A., & Wiley, W. W. (1973). *An introduction to functional job analysis: A scaling of selected tasks from the social welfare field (Methods for manpower analysis No. 4).* Kalamazoo, MI: W. E. Upjohn Institute for Employee Research.

Gatewood, R. D., & Schoenfeldt, L. F. (1977). Content validity and the EEOC: A useful alternative for selection. *Personnel Journal, 56*(10), 520–524.

Guion, R. M. (1965). *Personnel testing.* New York: McGraw-Hill.

McCormick, E. J., Jeanneret, P. R., & Mecham, R. C. (1972). A study of job characteristics and job dimensions as based on the Position Analysis Questionnaire (PAQ). *Journal of Applied Psychology, 56*(4), 347–368.

Muchinsky, P. M. (1990). *Psychology applied to work* (3rd ed.). Pacific Grove, CA: Brooks/Cole Publishing.

Siegel, L., & Lane, I. M. (1987). *Personnel and organizational psychology* (2nd ed.). Homewood, IL: Richard D. Irwin.

CHAPTER 5

MAKING SENSE OF SALARY SURVEYS

Raymond B. Weinberg

No area of HR management requires the use of research methods on a daily basis as consistently as compensation administration does. As part of an organization's reward structure, direct or cash compensation programs play an increasingly important role in strategic organizational development efforts. More and more, employees are being asked to share in the risks and rewards of the organization. At the same time, employers are seeking new ways to link direct compensation with the values and culture of the organization (Lawler, 1981).

A central issue in this linkage is the concept of equity. In the eyes of employees, equity is closely related to perceptions of fairness and consistency. How employees perceive equity affects their contributions to the organization and ultimately, whether or not they decide to stay with the organization.

Two types of equity are important (Adams, 1963). Internal equity, or how employees view their pay in relation to others, has an impact on both motivation and morale. Typically, employees' perceptions of equity revolve around four job content areas—skill, effort, responsibility, and working conditions—found in many job evaluation plans. Compounding the situation are employees' perceptions of internal equity on the basis of differences in individual performance levels and length of service (Adams, 1965).

Equally important is external equity, or how employees compare their pay to the rates of pay of similar positions in other organizations. External equity is a prime determinant of turnover. This chapter will focus on using research methods in the area of external equity. Specifically, it will focus on reviewing external equity for a single job. Whether an organization subscribes to traditional position-based pay systems (job evaluation) or new person-based pay systems (skill or knowledge-based pay), research methods are important for gathering and interpreting salary survey information for compensation administration purposes (Schuster & Zingheim, 1992).

The Salary Survey

Gathering market pricing information through surveys represents a form of the most basic applied HR research. Although the gathering and interpreting of market pricing information may involve the use of many precise statistical measures, HR managers must remember that it is not an exact science. Many judgments may be made, including selecting jobs to be surveyed, defining the relevant labor market, selecting the population to be surveyed, and determining what information is needed (Bjorndal & Ison, 1993).

The selection of jobs to be surveyed, called benchmark jobs, is of critical importance. Organizations seek consistent information for comparison purposes. The degree of match between benchmark jobs and market jobs is critical for consistency. Benchmark jobs typically

- Are readily definable,

- Are common in the workplace,

- Are stable over time,

- Have multiple incumbents,

- Cover a sizable portion of the employee population, and

- Represent all salary levels in the organization.

Benchmark jobs serve to anchor salary data to the relevant market and form a basis for comparison of similar jobs in different organizations. Comparison factors of benchmark jobs typically include the functions for which the job is responsible, the scope of the job, and the reporting level or organizational title. These factors assist the matching of benchmark jobs to survey jobs.

Defining the relevant labor market is just as critical. Generally, the relevant labor market includes (1) the geographic area(s) where an organization would expect to recruit all potential employees for a job, and (2) the geographical area(s) to which one would normally expect to lose employees in a particular job.

Markets may be

- Local

- Regional

- National

- International

- Industry

- Function

The relevant labor market may also be defined on the basis of other factors such as labor supply; competitors; profitability; and size as typically measured by sales, assets, or number of employees.

Determining how many organizations within the relevant labor market are to be surveyed is also a critical judgment. As with any research survey, the sample size must be large enough and sufficiently representative to draw conclusions regarding the total population.

Finally, the type of information sought is critical. Specific questions must be answered by the survey for it to be useful to the organization. The answers to these questions serve as a basis of understanding for the survey data.

This quest for information leaves an organization with four choices on gathering survey data:

- To obtain surveys that are available for purchase,

- To participate in sponsored surveys,

- To have custom third-party surveys conducted, or

- To conduct its own survey.

Factors to be considered in deciding which option to select include cost, time, reliability, confidentiality, and availability.

Understanding Survey Formats

Figure 5-1 is an excerpt from a compensation survey conducted by the Human Resource Association of the Midlands, a Society for Human Resource Management (SHRM) affiliated chapter in Omaha, Nebraska. It is an example of a sponsored survey. To use survey data, one must first fully understand the nature of the information being presented. Specifically, the explanations apply to Figure 5-1.

1. Firm Code: Most salary surveys guarantee participants anonymity and confidentiality regarding the information presented. For this particular survey, each participating organization is randomly assigned a code with which to identify its own data among the results of the other participating organizations. Participants do not know the codes of other responding organizations.

2. Firm Size Code: As previously mentioned, a consideration in selecting a relevant labor market may be size of organization used. Under the column Firm Size code, firms have been assigned a size code on the basis of total employee populations. Definitions of the groupings are in summary form for each job. For instance, in this case, the codes indicate the following: Group 1—100 to 250 employees; Group 2—251 to 750 employees; Group 3—750 to 1,500 employees; and Group 4—over 1,500 employees.

3. Number in Position: This column includes the total number of employees in each position as reported by each participating organization. Having information on number of incumbents in a position allows for calculating the weighted average salary level for the position.

4. Pay Data: Pay data are reported in three columns, representing the minimum, maximum, and actual average pay. Traditionally, nonexempt positions are reported as hourly rates and exempt positions are reported as annual rates. Usually, the developer of a survey converts raw data supplied by participants into hourly rates of pay for actual hours in a work week as reported by the firm to ensure a standard measure for comparison purposes. Minimum is the new hire start pay for the job, maximum is the top pay for which the position is entitled,

and average pay is the mean or straight average salary for all incumbents in the job by respondent. When viewed in relation to all respondents, average pay is often referred to as the market rate for the job.

5. Percentage of Weighted Market Average: This column provides a calculation of the reported actual data expressed as a percentage of the weighted average reported in the data summary for all respondents.

6. Summary of the Data: The data in this figure were compiled and analyzed based on the responses of all participants and on the four size groupings. The statistical calculations made on the salary data include the following:

- Number of Firms: The number of firms responding with matches to the survey or benchmark job.

- Average Firm Size: The average total employee population of the responding firms for the survey job. Many surveys will include "Ins. Data," which means that insufficient data were entered when there were fewer than a specified number of firms in the category. Sample size is important when one is relying on the representativeness of the data.

- Number of Incumbents: The total number of employees in each position is reported. This information is used in calculating the weighted average statistic.

- Percentage Exempt: Organizations vary significantly in their determinations of whether positions are exempt or nonexempt under the Fair Labor Standards Act. In this particular instance, all of the positions reported were nonexempt. However, on some survey forms, such as in Figure 5–1, the percentage of exempt reported is shown as the total number of exempt positions responses divided by the total responses, and the result is expressed as a percentage.

- Average Hours Per Week: Respondents provide information on the hours per week that represent a standard work week. The reported statistic is the average of all of the responses for the job and allows for converting raw data into a uniform standard when different work weeks are used by survey participants.

- Straight Average: The total of the responses divided by the total number of respondents. Participants are usually instructed to average employee rates for the match positions. This statistic is often referred to as the mean.

- Weighted Average: The total of all reported employee salaries divided by the total number of employees. The calculations are corrected for missing data points by excluding from the computations cases that did not report both salary rates and incumbents.

- 25th Percentile: The point at which 25% of the organizations reported lower pay than this rate. This statistic is also referred to as the first quartile.

- Median: The point at which 50% of the organizations reported pay below this point (50th percentile). Each employer average is treated equally in this particular survey. The data were not weighted according to the number of employees.

- 75th Percentile: The point at which 75% of the organizations reported pay below this point. This statistic is also referred to as the third quartile.

- Midpoint: The midpoint is not reported by respondents, but is a calculation. The midpoint of the range is calculated by adding the minimum and maximum and dividing by 2.

Interpreting Survey Data

Now that each element of the survey data has been defined, it is important to understand what each of the statistics indicates. Some general rules for interpreting survey data follow:

- Measures of central tendency, such as a mean (straight average) or median, are generally less affected by sampling variations when sample sizes are large. However, as sample sizes decrease, measures of central tendency can be adversely affected.

Figure 5–1. Compensation Survey Excerpt

(B14) - Material Handler   (Typically Nonexempt)
Loads and unloads trucks, railway cars, or aircraft. Moves material within a warehouse or storage facility to and from the loading platform by carrying, pushing, following, or using hand trucks or other material handling equipment.

Firm Code	Firm Size Group	Number in Position	Minimum	Maximum	Average Actual	Percentage of Wtd Mkt Avg (%)
73	2	7	4.25	6.00	4.95	55.6
48	1	6	6.22	8.89	6.72	75.5
45	2	2	6.45	8.55	6.89	77.4
92	4	30	5.86	8.89	7.03	79.0
97	3	109	6.78	9.38	7.26	81.6
93	4	13	7.23	9.77	7.40	83.1
105	1	3	6.00	9.50	7.62	85.6
94	1	3			7.75	87.1
53	4	8	7.07	10.61	8.48	95.3
28	2	22	7.15	9.25	8.60	96.6
115	3	37		9.29	9.29	104.4
101	4	39	7.99	10.78	10.03	112.7
42	3	3	7.98	12.14	10.49	117.9
4	4	6			10.55	118.5
9	4	2	7.50	10.82	10.84	121.8
78	1	7	8.30	11.85	11.45	128.7
11	2	2	8.36	11.60	11.60	130.3
67	4	54	11.30	12.73	12.44	139.8
57	3	4	12.60	15.75	14.77	166.0

Summary - (B14) - Material Handler (Figure 5–1 continued)

All Respondents

		Minimum	Midpoint	Maximum	Actual
# of Firms:	19				
Avg Firm Size:	2,067				
	Str Avg:	7.57	8.95	10.34	9.17
	Wtd Avg:	7.74	8.94	10.13	8.90
# of Incumbents:	357				
% Exempt:	5.3%				
Avg Hrs/Wk:	40.2				
	25th %tile:	6.39	7.82	9.25	7.33
	Median:	7.19	8.48	9.77	8.60
	75th %tile:	8.07	9.83	11.60	10.70

Group 1: 1 to 250 Employees

		Minimum	Midpoint	Maximum	Actual
# of Firms:	4				
Avg Firm Size:	139				
# of Incumbents:	19				
	Str Avg:	6.84	8.46	10.08	8.39
	Wtd Avg:	7.09	8.70	10.30	8.77
	Median:	6.22	7.86	9.50	7.69

Group 2: 251 to 750 Employees

		Minimum	Midpoint	Maximum	Actual
# of Firms:	4				
Avg Firm Size:	476				
# of Incumbents:	33				
	Str Avg:	6.55	7.70	8.85	8.01
	Wtd Avg:	6.57	7.62	8.66	7.90
	Median:	6.80	7.85	8.90	7.75

Group 3: 751 to 1,5000 Employees

		Minimum	Midpoint	Maximum	Actual
# of Firms:	4				
Avg Firm Size:	1,049				
# of Incumbents:	153				
	Str Avg:	9.12	10.38	11.64	10.45
	Wtd Avg:	7.01	8.30	9.58	8.01
	Median:	7.98	9.37	10.76	9.89

Group 4: Over 1,500 Employees

		Minimum	Midpoint	Maximum	Actual
# of Firms:	7				
Avg Firm Size:	4,659				
# of Incumbents:	152				
Str Avg:		7.83	9.21	10.60	9.54
Wtd Avg:		8.65	9.83	11.01	10.02
Median:		7.37	9.03	10.70	10.03

Bonus Information:
% Eligible: 21.1%   Avg Bonus: 6.4%   (Among 5 Reporting Bonus Data)

Note. From a compensation survey conducted by the Human Resource Association of the Midlands, a SHRM-affiliated chapter in Omaha, Nebraska.

• As one reviews salary survey data, if a significant difference exists between average or mean and median statistics, it can be the result of a sample skewed high or low caused by a few unusual cases. Means are generally affected by a skewed sample, whereas medians are not. The use of a mean or median is a matter of preference. Usually, if there is a high degree of confidence in the sampling, the median is the preferred estimate of the typical pay for a job, because it minimizes the effect of extremely high or low data values.

• In Figure 5–1, in addition to the mean, which is reported as average actual, there is a weighted mean. The use of a weighted mean implies giving equal weight to every employee represented in the survey sample, whereas the use of a straight mean implies giving equal weight to each company represented in the sample. These two methods of comparison, mean and weighted mean, should not be combined. On the one hand, if the survey data and sources are very well-specified and defined, the use of a weighted mean is the statistic of choice as being most representative of the market rate for a job. On the other hand, if a less well-defined survey is being used, such as a broad-based national survey, the use of an unweighted mean would be most representative of the market rate.

• In addition to measures of central tendency, it is important to consider the dispersion or range of the data. The most accurate way of measuring dispersion is through the use of standard deviation. However, in most published surveys, standard deviations are not calculated. In Figure 5–1, dispersion is calculated by the ordering of the average salaries and the computation of percentile ranges from lowest to highest in an array. In this case, percentile ranges are reported at the 25th percentile and the 75th percentile in addition to the median (50th percentile). Unless there are large numbers of data points, such as 15 or more, the use of percentiles other than the median may not be appropriate. For large numbers of data points, percentiles have more meaning.

• Another meaningful measure is interquartile range. It is the difference between the third quartile (75th percentile) and the first quartile (25th percentile). It is the range of the middle 50% of the data.

Conclusion

This chapter illustrates a number of research approaches for reviewing salary survey data for a single job to determine market competitiveness. More involved measures and statistical applications are available for reviewing a range of jobs or a salary structure, but such methods go beyond the scope of this chapter.

As previously stated, salary surveys are not precise, but they do require the use of sound, consistent judgment. Individual salary survey data are often subject to fickle behavior from year to year, and aberrations are common. Surveys are retrospective and cannot replace vigilance in keeping on top of market trends. Research methodologies are useful in evaluating competitiveness and can assist HR practitioners as they establish a rewards structure for an organization.

References and Suggested Readings

Adams, J. S. (1963). Toward an understanding of inequity. *Journal of Abnormal Psychology, 67*(5), 422–436.

Adams, J. S. (1965). Inequity in social exchange. In I. Berkowitz (Ed.), *Advances in experimental psychology.* Orlando, FL: Academic Press.

Bjorndal, J. A., & Ison, L. (1993). *Mastering market data: An approach to analyzing and applying salary survey information.* Scottsdale, AZ: American Compensation Association.

Lawler, E. E., III. (1981). *Pay and organizational development.* Reading, MA: Addison-Wesley.

Lawler, E. E., III. (1990). *Strategic pay: Aligning organizational strategies and pay systems.* San Francisco: Jossey-Bass.

Rich, J. R., & Phalen, C. C. (1992–1993, Winter). A framework for the design of total compensation surveys. *ACA Journal,* 18–29.

Schuster, J. R., & Zingheim, P. K. (1992). *The new pay: Linking employee and organizational performance.* New York: Lexington Books.

Wallace, M. L., & Fay, C. H. (1983). *Compensation theory and practice.* Boston: Kent Publishing.

CHAPTER 6

PERFORMANCE APPRAISALS

Lynda L. Brown

Most organizations have an official feedback mechanism called performance appraisal. The goal of any performance appraisal system is to effectively evaluate the work performance of employees. While measuring work performance has traditionally been linked to compensation and rewards, information from appraisals is valuable in other HR activities, including performance management, feedback, documentation, staffing decisions, organizing work, training needs assessment, and research and evaluation of HR programs. Performance appraisals have also become an important factor in lawsuits, where they are the most heavily litigated personnel practice today.

What Is the Value of Measuring Performance?

Work performance has been defined as "a record of outcomes produced on a specific job function or activity during a specified time period" (Bernardin & Russell, 1993, p. 379). By measuring work performance, employers can provide feedback on behaviors that need modifying or changing, determine potential for advancement, reward performance equitably, and assess employees' development needs.

What Is Being Measured?

For performance appraisals to be effective, organizations must clearly define what they are trying to measure and why. Because it is such an important management tool, performance measurement should be tailored to an organization's needs. An organization should start with its strategic plan to design an appraisal system consistent with the philosophy and goals of the organization. The design includes measurement content and measurement process.

Content includes the focus (person-centered, work-centered, or outcomes-centered), types of criteria, and use of performance level descriptors (e.g., anchors or benchmarks such as "satisfactorily," "rarely," "exceeds").

Identifying performance means determining what areas are to be studied and by whom. A job analysis is a critical source of information on the dimensions of work performance. The job analysis is a systematic examination of the knowledge, skills, and abilities required for a job and for the duties and responsibilities of that job. The job analysis is used to develop a job description that delineates the work to be performed and job specifications that outline the requirements for accomplishing the job. Job descriptions and specifications need to be behavior—as well as results—oriented. Expected standards of performance for each element of work need to be defined. Individual or team performance should be measured against those standards.

The rater in some way "observes" the employee's performance and makes a value judgment as to "how good" it is. Feeling the effects of competition and the need to focus on customer satisfaction, organizations are concerned with not only *what* the ratee gets done but also *how*. The measurement tools, therefore, must enable the rater to observe and measure behaviors as well as results.

Traditionally, raters evaluated the ratee's personal performance level without accounting for any situational influences that have either a positive or negative impact on performance. Increasingly, raters must look at performance from a systems perspective, as organizations acknowledge that much variance in performance is related to system, not person, variables.

Who Does the Measuring?

Typically, supervisors are the source of information about the quality and quantity of work performed by their subordinates. Changes in organizational structures and objectives (e.g., matrix organizations, self-managed work teams, reengineering, and total quality management) have created the need for alternative or additional sources of information. As the purpose of measurement shifts from salary decisions to performance improvement on both an individual and organizational level, more organizations are using "360-degree feedback" or other multi-rater appraisal systems, where raters include supervisors, project managers, peers, subordinates, customers and clients, and employees themselves.

There are differences in job knowledge, the way information is processed, and motivation among the various types of raters. Although research shows a lack of convergence among ratings from different sources, an advantage of multi-rater systems is that each of the sources of information about performance provides a unique perspective, so that the sources complement one another, providing greater reliability and a more complete picture of outcomes as well as the behaviors that influence outcomes. A disadvantage of using several sources of appraisal information is the complexity and the time-consuming process of data collection, analysis, and rater training. Nevertheless, 360-degree and multi-rater systems are enjoying greater popularity and are piquing the interest of many HR professionals in search of improved performance measurement techniques. Regardless of whether one or more rater types is used, it is important to understand the strengths and weaknesses of each appraisal source.

Supervisors, the most traditional and frequent source of information about work performance, have access to information about outcomes and behavior because they can observe the actual performance of the work and the work products. They are most likely to be involved in the job analysis, development of the job description and job specifications, and selection of the employee being evaluated. Increasingly, supervisors are encouraged to rely less heavily on outcomes and to balance outcomes with behaviors that are critical to achieving desired results. Supervisors are criticized for their tendency to hold the ratee accountable for all performance, without considering the system or situational factors. Organizations that continue to rely on supervisor evaluations should redesign measures and methodology and should provide rater training if both outcomes and behaviors are to receive necessary attention.

Until recently, self-ratings have not been widely adopted. In their assessments of themselves, employees often rely more heavily on their work behaviors (e.g., effort expended) rather than on actual results, but they often have more accurate information about their own performance than do other raters, even supervisors. In contrast to supervisors, self-raters may be more inclined to attribute performance to the situation—to system factors—especially if the outcome does not measure up to their perceived effort or contribution. As organizations interested in fostering teamwork and employee involvement become interested in using self-rating, researchers are looking at ways to improve the quality of self-ratings.

Like self-ratings, peer ratings have grown in popularity in this new organizational environment. Research has shown that peer ratings are more predictive of future success than either self-ratings or supervisor ratings, probably because peers look at both outcomes and behaviors. Peers may also be more sensitive to factors in the system that have an impact on performance and to the ability of the ratee to affect system factors. Peer evaluations are criticized because of concerns about lack of experience, training, and proper motivation (e.g., friendship or, alternatively, competition among co-workers).

Subordinate ratings are widely accepted in leadership research and organizational development theory but have just begun to gain acceptance in most organizations. Subordinates as raters are subject to the same criticisms as peers: lack of training or experience as raters and questionable motivational processes. Another criticism of subordinate ratings is that they may be too heavily influenced by behaviors rather than outcomes, possibly because subordinates are not in a position to accurately observe or assess the final products or services for which the supervisor is responsible.

The use of customer feedback is one of the trademarks of the Total Quality Management movement. Because of the focus on service and quality as outcomes, the customer rather than the supervisor, co-worker, or employee may be the best source of information. The client or customer can be internal or external to the organization. Customer evaluations can be an effective organizational development tool and help employees focus attention on customer satisfaction rather than supervisor satisfaction alone. One difficulty is that customers tend to be influenced by system factors. For example, rating customer service centers negatively when the real problem is with the product design that required the customer to make the return or to use the service center. The challenge is to design customer appraisals that assess performance independent of system factors.

The goal of appraisals is accurate ratings. Therefore, choosing the rater source should be a function of the purpose of the appraisal, the various motivational differences among raters, the experience and training of raters, and their access to and ability to process information about the work performance of the ratee. Regardless of who measures an employee's performance, major criticisms of evaluation systems are that they are not accurate because of rater inexperience, accountability, or bias.

Evaluations can be biased because of a number of perceptual errors on the part of the rater. Rating errors include leniency or strictness, central tendency, halo effect, rater effect (including stereotypes), perceptual set, and primacy and recency effects. Leniency or strictness is the tendency to go easy or be tough on others, respectively. Generally that means that the rater restricts the range of ratings across the points on a scale rather than using the full range of possible scores. Central tendency errors occur when the rater tends to put all ratees toward the middle of the rating scale rather than to use either extreme. With the "halo" effect, the rater's overall impression of the ratee or the evaluation of the ratee on a dimension that is particularly important to the rater colors the evaluation on other specific dimensions of performance. When raters let their judgment be influenced by stereotypes or perceptual sets, they tend to ignore individual differences and to lump employees into categories based on a few traits or characteristics. Attitudes toward the ratee, rather than actual behaviors or results, form the basis for the rating. Primacy and recency errors are the result of weighing incidents more heavily or of information that depends on circumstances early in the appraisal period or on ones that are very recent.

Other problems of rater accuracy relate to observation of performance. Whatever the measure, there needs to be a standard against which judgments can be compared. It is clear from the research and from actual practice that there are both objective and subjective standards. Whatever the criteria or scales, employee perceptions and reactions to appraisals are important for appraisals to be effective. Any system is doomed to fail when dissatisfaction among ratees and perceptions of unfairness and inaccuracy exist. Unfortunately, some organizations attempt to solve this problem by merely altering the appraisal format rather than by examining the entire appraisal system. While not the sole solution to ineffective evaluation systems, training of both raters and ratees is an important part of the process. Training is effective at enhancing awareness and improving rater observational and categorization skills, thereby increasing accuracy and consistency.

What Methods Are Used to Evaluate Performance?

Performance appraisal may be formal or informal. Most organizations require a formal evaluation at least once a year and generally use the information for compensation. Informal appraisals focus more on communication, may be brief (e.g., the "1-minute manager" approach), and generally occur more frequently than formal appraisals. While both objective and subjective approaches are used to measure performance, objective measures based on behaviors or results are more useful, equitable, and legally defensible. Objective measures evaluate performance against specific standards; subjective measures are helpful when assessing desired characteristics that are harder to quantify (e.g., management potential, communication skills, teamwork, etc.).

The method and rating instrument should be based on the work performance data that are available to be measured; the purpose of the measurement; and whether it is legally defensible, fits with the strategic goals, and minimizes rater errors. Behaviorally oriented methods include checklists, field review, graphic rating scales, forced choice, critical incidents, assessment centers, and behaviorally anchored rating. Comparison methods include ranking, forced distribution, and paired comparisons. Results-oriented methods include management by objectives and work planning and review (WP&R). Increasingly, group results, not just individual results, are being measured and linked to productivity improvement and results-sharing compensation practices.

A national study of current and projected future practices in performance assessment shows overall ratings will become less important in the future, as will numerical rankings and forced rankings. This trend is due in part to research indicating that appraisal systems are more effective if they are more specific in content (systems requiring ratings on each relevant criterion for each activity rather than stating a single overall judgment). Forced rankings, such as where employees are rated according to a predetermined percentage of ratings distributions, will see the biggest drop in use.

What Administrative Factors Influence Effective Performance Measurement?

Whatever the format for performance measurement, factors influencing success include management support, communication, clear objectives, rater accountability, and the specifics of the process itself. Especially critical are control of rater errors (discussed above), clear definition of raters and ratees, frequency and timing of performance feedback, tools for collecting the information, feedback methods, and evaluation of the process.

There is growing debate about the value and role of traditional annual appraisals and their primary link to compensation. If the goal is to motivate an employee to improve performance and to set goals for improvement, traditional measurement tools may not be as effective as frequent observation, coaching, and WP&R. Measures of performance must align with other major organizational systems such as compensation, rewards and recognition, management information, promotion and succession planning, and organizational communication. An effective performance measurement system will identify developmental needs; facilitate decision making about recognition, rewards, and compensation; ensure that employees have clear goals and a sense of purpose; increase communication; and incorporate behaviors and dimensions or competencies that are critical to organizational success (Rogers, Miller, & Worklan, 1993).

References and Suggested Readings

Appraising performance appraisal. (1991). (Harvard Business Review Paperback No. 90070). Boston: Harvard Business School.

Anthony, W. R., Perrewe, P. L., & Kacmar, K. M. (1993). *Strategic human resource management*. New York: Harcourt, Brace, Javonovich.

Berk, R. A. (1986). *Performance assessment*. Baltimore: Johns Hopkins University Press.

Bernardin, J. J., & Russell, J. A. (1993). *Human resource management: An experiential approach*. New York: McGraw-Hill.

Cardy, R. L., & Dobbins, G. (1994). *Performance appraisal: Alternative perspectives*. Cincinnati, OH: South-Western Publishing.

Lawler, E. E., Mohrman, A. M., & Resnick, S. M. (1984, Summer). Performance appraisal revisited. *Organizational Dynamics, 13*(1), 20–35.

Mohrman, A. M., Resnick-West, S. M., & Lawler, E. E. (1989). *Designing performance appraisal systems*. San Francisco: Jossey-Bass.

Rogers, R. W., Miller, L. P, & Worklan, J. (1993). *Performance management: What's hot—what's not*. Washington, DC: Development Dimensions International and the Society for Human Resource Management.

CHAPTER 7

EMPLOYEE TURNOVER: ANALYZING EMPLOYEE MOVEMENT OUT OF THE ORGANIZATION

Carolyn Wiley

Introduction

Unplanned employee turnover is a strategic managerial concern. When an employee leaves, an organization usually experiences substantial costs. Turnover costs U.S. industry an estimated $11 billion a year. In particular, Merck & Company found that, depending on the job, turnover costs were 1.5 to 2.5 times the annual salary paid. Corning tallied its out-of-pocket turnover expenses (i.e., interview costs) and found them to be $16 to $18 million annually. These turnover costs may be placed in three broad categories: separation, replacement, and training costs. Separation costs include administrative costs related to employee termination, separation pay, and increased unemployment tax. Replacement costs include entrance interviews, testing, moving expenses, and medical exams. Training costs include orientation or informational literature, formal training programs, and on-the-job training. Perhaps the major cost associated with turnover is reduced productivity during the learning period.

Other consequences of turnover relate to the smoothness and continuity of organizational operations, employee morale, and the difficulty of replacing the departed employee. As a result, organizations are concerned about monitoring turnover, determining the variables that influence it, and managing turnover behavior.

Application

The main reason for measuring turnover costs is to improve management decision making. Knowing the extent and cost of employee turnover is important in securing funds, resources, and organizational commitment, which all reduce turnover. The first step in measuring turnover is to define it generally as a permanent movement out of the organization. It can be considered the net result of the exit and entrance of employees from and into the organization.

Turnover Rates. Statistically, turnover is usually computed as the number of employee separations divided by the total number in the workforce, expressed as a percentage, as illustrated below.

$$\frac{\text{Number of employee separations during the month}}{\text{Total number of employees at mid month}} \times 100$$

Thus, an organization with 20 separations (employees who leave the organization from January 1 to 31) and 200 employees as of January 15 (mid-month) has a monthly turnover or separation rate of 10% (20/200 = 10%). This computation of separation or turnover rates is recommended by the Department of Labor.

Turnover rates vary among industries, organizations, geographic locations, departments, and occupations, as well as by employee characteristics such as age, education, and organizational tenure. For example, younger, newer, unskilled, and blue-collar employees tend to have higher turnover rates than do contrasting groups. For this reason, turnover should be calculated for various categories of interest, as well as for the organization as a whole. For instance, an organization may not have a severe organization-wide turnover rate, but may have a severe departmental turnover rate or a high professional employee turnover rate, which would require appropriate action to alleviate the problem. The turnover rates for subgroups such as these can be computed using the formula above. Once computed, the turnover rate can be compared with previous rates for the same periods, with the rates of other organizations, and with the national average obtained from the U.S. Bureau of Labor Statistics. For comparisons of turnover data, the *Monthly Labor Review* and the BNA *Quarterly Report on Job Absence and Turnover* are useful sources.

Avoidable Separations Turnover Rates. Calculating the turnover for *avoidable separations* is another, more refined, method for computing the turnover rate. This method yields the most significant measure of the effectiveness of a HR program because it represents the portion of employee turnover that management has the most opportunity to control. To compute this type of turnover, the *unavoidable separations*—those over which the organization normally has no control (e.g., maternity and paternity leaves, return to school, illness, death, marriage, or spousal relocation)—are deducted from the total separations for a given period. This remainder is divided by the total mid-month workforce to determine the avoidable separation turnover rate.

$$\frac{\text{Total separations in selected period} - \text{unavoidable separations}}{\text{Total number of employees at mid month or average workforce}} \times 100$$

In the previous example, if 6 of the 20 separations were unavoidable, the 14 remaining separations divided by 200 employees yields a 7% avoidable turnover rate.

One problem with the turnover rates already discussed is that they mask the usual higher turnover of newer employees. One approach to studying the turnover of newer employees is to compute their *survivor* or *wastage rates*. This is done by computing the proportion of new employees who stay or leave during a given time period. For example, if 25 employees are hired 1 month and 15 of them are still employed after 3 months, their survival rate is 60% (or wastage rate of 40%).

Not only is the quantitative rate of turnover important, but also the quality of personnel leaving an organization is important.

Turnover Reduction Strategies. Turnover represents more than a monetary loss. Indeed, those who leave may be the company's most valued human resources. Because of the impact such employees have on an organization, special attention should be given to whether the turnover is functional (beneficial to the organization) or dysfunctional (losing a valuable employee). Specifically, sufficient attention should be given to turnover among managers, professional personnel, and those employees possessing unique skills. Replacing these employees can be expensive and time consuming. A company turnover reduction program may include one of, or a combination of, the following strategies. A strategy such as realistic job previews (RJPs) can reduce cognitive dissonance, which is the difference between what newcomers expect and what they find. The higher the dissonance the more likely the employee is to quit. In addition to RJPs, other strategies such as fair pay systems and opportunities for career advancement can be incorporated into the company's turnover reduction program. The following are suggested turnover reduction strategies:

1. Realistic job previews

2. Improved selection

3. Good employee orientation

4. Appropriate training

5. Supervisory leadership

6. Well-designed employee mentoring systems

7. Equitable or fair pay systems

8. Improved working conditions

9. Job redesign

10. Opportunities for career advancement

11. Communication

12. Data analysis

Analysis

To apply the most appropriate turnover reduction strategies, management must first determine the cause of turnover behavior. To facilitate this, management needs to establish appropriate turnover categories. For example, turnover can be classified as involuntary or voluntary. Involuntary turnover occurs when an employee is discharged or terminated, often for just cause. Voluntary turnover occurs when an employee leaves by the employee's own choice, and such turnover can be caused by a number of factors such as poor job feedback, job dissatisfaction, unmet job expectations, performance problems, situational constraints, socialization difficulties, greater degrees of job stress, and a lack of career advancement opportunities.

After computing appropriate turnover rates, an organization frequently can determine the reasons for employee separations by compiling and comparing the results of exit interviews by employee group, department, division, and so on. An example of an exit interview is given in Figure 7–1.

Questionnaires may be used to study turnover. Turnover factors can be listed on the questionnaires, and respondents (former employees) can be asked to indicate how much influence each factor had on their decision to leave the organization. From this type of study, management can determine what probably caused employees to quit and whether the most influential factors are controllable to some degree.

Attitudinal surveys may be used to study turnover by including sections on current employees' intention to quit and on employees' future plans with the organization. To obtain data on employees' intentions, the organization may decide to ask the following:

"How often have you seriously considered quitting your present job?"

a. Never

b. Seldom

c. Occasionally

d. Often

e. All the time

To obtain data pertaining to employees' future plans, the organization may ask the following:

"What are your future plans regarding staying with our organization?"

a. Definitely do not intend to stay

b. Plan to stay until I find a better job

c. Plan to stay unless personal or medical situation changes

d. Plan to stay indefinitely

Figure 7–1. Exit Interview

Name: _____

Position: _____

Supervisor: _____

Hire Date: _____ Termination Date: _____

What made you decide to leave your current job? (Check all that apply)

Primary   Secondary

❑   ❑   Secured better job

❑   ❑   Return to school

❑   ❑   Family

❑   ❑   Issues with supervisor

❑   ❑   Problems with hours

❑   ❑   Not satisfied with wages

❑   ❑   Disliked type of work

❑   ❑   Professional level of job

❑   ❑   Quantity of work

❑   ❑   Physical conditions

❑   ❑   Working conditions

❑   ❑   Transportation problems

❑   ❑   Lack of advancement opportunities

❑   ❑   Other _____

Figure 7-1 (*continued*)

What did you like *most* about your job?

What did you like *least* about your job?

Do you feel training opportunities were made available to you?

Yes ❑   No ❑   Comments _____

Do you think your current supervisor was fair and reasonable? If not, please explain.

Yes ❑   No ❑   Comments _____

Do you believe you were given access to and realistic consideration for promotional opportunities within the organization?

Yes ❑   No ❑   Comments _____

Do you feel your contributions were appreciated by your supervisor and others?

Yes ❑   No ❑   Comments _____

Did you have the appropriate equipment and resources necessary to perform your job?

Yes ❑   No ❑   Comments _____

Figure 7-1 (*continued*)

Was your salary satisfactory for the job you were performing?

   Yes ❏ No ❏   Comments _____

Were you satisfied with the employee benefits provided?

   Yes ❏ No ❏   Comments _____

Was the physical working environment comfortable and conducive to productivity?

   Yes ❏ No ❏   Comments _____

Was the job realistically presented to you when you were hired or most recently changed positions?

   Yes ❏ No ❏   Comments _____

Do you have any suggestions for improvement?

Are there any changes that could have been made to prevent you from leaving?

Other comments, if any:

Date Discussed:_____ Interviewer: _____

Note. From SHRM Information Center, 1996.

These employees' responses can be further examined to determine whether they are correlated with performance, pay, tenure with the organization, or job satisfaction. The Job Description Index (work and supervisory satisfaction scales) and the General Satisfaction Scale (from the Job Diagnostic Survey) are commonly used instruments designed to measure job-related satisfaction.

Turnover on a specific job may be explored through employee task-related self-esteem to determine whether employees leave because they perceive themselves to be incompetent. To do this, an organization can use organizational position or job descriptions to identify activities considered critical to a given job. After a list of activities is developed, the organization can ask the respondents to rate their ability levels.

Developing profiles of employees who turn over at various times during employment can generate useful information for the organization. Employee records can be used to collect data on employees who leave the company at particular times. Critical characteristics of these employees (obtained by reviewing the distributions of their age, employment time, salary, and recruitment source) can be used to describe those who leave in 6 months versus those who leave in 12 months, 24 months, or 36 months. Similar profiles can be developed for dichotomous groups of "leavers" and "stayers" in each department or division of the organization. This information is especially useful if the profiles reveal characteristics or factors that significantly distinguish one group from the other. If the "stayers" in a particular job (e.g., receptionist) have higher educational levels, managers may want to reevaluate the position or its educational requirements and change the job specification.

References and Suggested Readings

Cascio, W. F. (1995). *Managing human resources: Productivity, quality of work life, profits* (4th ed.). New York: McGraw-Hill.

Cotton, J. L., & Tuttle, J. M. (1986). Employee turnover: A meta analysis and review with implications for research. *Academy of Management Review, 11*(1), 55–70.

Darden, W. R., Hampton, R. D., & Boatwright, E. W. (1987). Investigating retail employee turnover: An application of survival analysis. *Journal of Retailing, 63*(1), 69–88.

Employee turnover: Measurement and control. (1987). *Compensation and Benefits Review, 19*(4), 64–74.

Gaertner, J. P., Hemmeter, P. E., & Pitman, M. K. (1987). Employee turnover in public accounting: A new perspective. *CPA Journal, 57*(2), 34–37.

Ivancevich, J. M. (1995). *Human resource management* (6th ed.). Chicago: Richard D. Irwin.

Jackofsky, E. F., Ferris, K. R., & Breckenridge, B. G. (1986). Evidence for a curvilinear relationship between job performance and turnover. *Journal of Management, 12*(1), 105–111.

Job absence and turnover control. (1981, October). *The Personnel Policies Forum Survey No. 132* (pp. 66–68). Washington, DC: Bureau of National Affairs, Inc.

Lucas, G. H., Jr., Parasuraman, A., Davis, R. A., & Enis, B. M. (1987). An empirical study of salesforce turnover. *Journal of Marketing, 51*(3), 34–59.

Mathis, R. L., & Jackson, J. H. (1988). *Personnel/human resource management.* St. Paul, MN: West Publishing.

McEvoy, G. M., & Cascio, W. F.(1985). Strategies for reducing employee turnover: A meta-analysis. *Journal of Applied Psychology, 70*(2), 342–353.

O'Connor, E. J., Pooyan, A., Weekley, J., Peters, L. H., Frank, B., & Erenkrantz, B. (1984). Situational constraint effects on performance, affective reactions, and turnover: A field replication and extension. *Journal of Applied Psychology, 69*(4), 663–672.

Schultz, R. M., Bigoness, W. J., & Gagnon, J. P. (1987). Research note: Determinants of turnover intentions among retail pharmacists. *Journal of Retailing, 63*(1), 89–98.

Sherman, A. W., Jr., Bohlander, G. W., & Chruden, H. J. (1988). *Managing human resources.* Cincinnati, OH: South-Western Publishing.

CHAPTER 8

CONDUCTING A TRAINING
NEEDS ASSESSMENT

Jeannette Swist

A review of the literature indicates that training programs are often prescribed as the drug of choice for problem situations in organizations. How often have you heard, "We've got a training problem ..." or "They're not doing it the way they're supposed to ..."? Often these statements are only *symptoms* of a problem. Until the problem is understood in greater detail, proposing a solution or an intervention can be a costly and fruitless endeavor. Often overlooked as the first step in the performance improvement process is the training needs assessment. A *need* is not a want or desire. It is a gap between "what is" and "what ought to be." The needs assessment serves to identify the gaps, and it considers whether the problem can be solved by training. The assessment is part of a planning process focusing on identifying and solving performance problems.

Why Conduct a Training Needs Assessment?

A needs assessment is important because it helps the HR practitioner

- To determine which training is relevant to your employees' jobs,

- To determine which training will improve performance,

- To determine whether training will make a difference,

- To distinguish training needs from organizational problems, and

- To link improved job performance with the organization's goals and bottom line.

In reading different articles and books, you will come across the words *need assessment* and *need analysis*. The terms are interchangeable, but they have the same meaning and purpose—to assess and analyze. The primary purpose of the training needs assessment-analysis process is to ensure that there is a need for training and to identify the nature of the content for the training program. Conducting an assessment is a way to collect information that can be used to decide what type of development will be perceived as relevant and useful. An assessment enables a conversation to take place that questions what skills and knowledge are required to be more effective. It is important that we view training or performance improvement efforts as a "system," not a "silo." Our efforts to improve one part of the organizational system will affect other jobs in the workplace environment. The needs assessment process is an important first step in the development of a training program or performance improvement initiatives.

A needs assessment provides an opportunity to consult with a variety of people in the organization. The information collected, the ideas generated, and the conversations that take place when people discuss their work lives lend enthusiasm to the process. The data collected—whether obtained through interviews, observations, focus groups, performance data, questionnaires, or tests—can clarify issues and provide a focus on performance.

Needs Assessment Methods: Scenarios

The format of a needs assessment can vary. Generally, an assessment is conducted as a survey. However, you may develop questions and conduct individual interviews or focus groups. Or you can collect and analyze performance data to determine common needs. We will explore these areas primarily through the use of personal observations; additional assessments may include on-site observation, testing, and assessment centers. On-site observations should be conducted by individuals who are experienced and knowledgeable with regard to performing a *task analysis* of the work processes, procedures, methods, and practices being observed. These individuals are referred to as subject matter experts (SMEs), and they can be found both inside and outside the organization. Typically, SMEs are individuals who once worked in the position and have the in-depth knowledge of the concepts and processes. Subject matter experts offer the troubleshooting information you may need to determine whether additional training is needed, or whether the situation is indicative of a needed intervention. If you plan to use testing and assessment centers, or both, you will want to check into validation and reliability studies to ensure compliance with legal requirements.

Scenario One—Surveying Needs. Let's say you work for a small to mid-size company and the president calls you into the office and says, "The organization has identified projected business goals, and we need be certain that (1) our management team understands the implications on an operational level, and (2) we get feedback to ascertain what types of assistance we need to give to our managers to support their needs." Consider the use of a questionnaire for this *organizational analysis*. Figure 8–1 gives an example.

Figure 8–1. Operational Effectiveness Survey

Please answer each question below by responding with your comment in the space provided:

1. Do you feel the vision of where _____ is going over the next several years has been communicated to the management team?

   Yes ____   No ____

2a. If yes, describe in a few words what your understanding is of that vision.

2b. By what means was the message communicated?

3. Identify the three most important strengths _____ brings to our customers.

Figure 8–1 (*continued*)

4. What three things must _____ do better to be a leader among our competition in the marketplace?

5. To become the most valuable supplier to our customers, _____ must

6. In your opinion, who are the three main competitors of _____?

7. **From a customer perspective,** what do you think are the most important measures of our success?

8. **From an internal perspective,** what do you think are the most important measures of our success?

9. If you were going to start up a national competitor to _____, what are the three most significant things you would do differently?

10. Rank the following strategic issues from 1 (most important) to 7 (least important):

_____ Improved information system

_____ Improved product or service pricing

_____ Customer service effectiveness

_____ Explicit corporate vision

_____ Defined goals and objectives

_____ Improved process performance measurement

_____ Total Quality Management

Figure 8–1 (*continued*)

---

11. The last time you had a personal performance evaluation was _____.

12. If you have had a performance review, do you recall whether you were able to discuss needs and issues at that review?

13. What should an orientation program for new managers include?

14. What three key activities should we work to improve over the next 2 to 3 years?

15. Can you identify any training needs that would help you in meeting the operational goals of your unit?

A survey of this type provides both qualitative and quantitative data for planning purposes. It also says to members of the management team that the organization wants them to succeed. If the survey, results, and subsequent feedback are used to determine training content or operational level changes, managers will feel that their input helped human resources facilitate the change effort.

Scenario Two—Interviewing Methods. What do you do when department managers want a training program to solve what they think is a problem? Is training the answer? If training is the answer, what content should be covered?

Is the problem centering on an individual performer level or on a joint work-in-progress level? This situation may best be served by conducting a problem analysis interview. First, set up a time to meet with the department manager. Prepare for that meeting by developing open-ended questions to determine more completely what the manager believes should be happening, as well as to understand the current situation. Here are some examples:

1. Describe the situation you have encountered.

2. What do you observe that indicates there is a problem? What specifically is the performer doing wrong? Doing right?

3. Probe frequency: *How often* does it occur? Probe location: *Where* does it occur? Probe timing: *When* is it a problem? Probe longevity: *How long* has it been a problem? Probe identity: *Who* is the performer in question? Probe desired performance: *What* is the desired performance? Probe who else is affected: *What or who else* is affected by the performer? Probe cost value of discrepancy: *How much* is the problem costing the organization?

4. What are some of the reasons you think training is needed?

5. What is the result you are seeking from a training intervention?

6. If I were to go out and talk to the employee(s) involved, what would they say?

Keep in mind that we are conditioned to ask questions about things that are not working well—the problems—so that we can fix them. Try to find out about the successes—what has worked? In a consulting assignment with a floor-tile manufacturer who wanted to decrease the number of loss-time incidents, we suggested what that firm considered to be quite innovative: interviewing employees who have been accident-free since their last incident so we could learn what they have done differently. Also, consider the on-site observation as a secondary data-gathering method. Remember, the SME can be of great assistance in regard to work processes, procedures, methods, and practices being observed. For example, you might bring in an SME to perform a safety assessment of the plant operations and a task analysis of the work being performed on the line.

Training is not a panacea. What is occurring in the department may be only a symptom, and treating it with a training program may be only a "Band-Aid approach" at best.

Scenario Three—Data Gathering. With the continuing emphasis on competency development, companies are seeking individuals who consistently meet or exceed performance requirements and organizational goals. In turn, more and more companies are turning to 360-degree feedback, also referred to as multi-rater assessments (MRA), and to testing or assessment centers. These tools play a key part in a training needs assessment from the standpoint of a continuous improvement process!

The first source of acquiring assessment information is to define the abilities desired of managers—competencies, knowledge, skills, tasks, behaviors, and actions. This has been the function of job analysis and the resulting job descriptions. As companies continue to go through change, these analyses and descriptions require continuous updating. However, these descriptions become the basis for evaluating levels of competence, which can help HR practitioners to assess needs for training and development programs. These descriptions are one source of assessment information.

A second source of assessment information has been performance evaluation data. The purpose of evaluation was to help individuals to enhance those areas needing improvement. The difficult task of assessing how well people are doing their jobs has traditionally fallen to supervisors and managers, even though they are usually not in the best position to observe employee performance on a regular basis. More companies are turning to MRAs or 360-degree feedbacks. This technological evolution has a profound implication. *Managers now have a tool for separating the evaluation of abilities for developmental purposes from the evaluation of performance results!* MRAs involve identifying key direct reports (such as peers, internal customers, the employee's manager, subordinates, and the employee's manager's manager) to participate in a performance evaluation. An MRA is an assessment tool that involves each employee in developing a performance enhancement plan. From this information, companies can identify potential training programs and can track and evaluate progress.

A third source of information may be for the company to use a managerial evaluation or assessment center to develop individuals in career pathing or a succession planning process. There are tests and assessment center processes that assess skills, aptitudes, and behaviors for specific jobs. Through administration, the company would receive objective feedback on which candidates currently possess needed characteristics, or on certain developmental areas necessary for candidates in a career path or succession plan. Some of the typical functions assessed for managerial level candidates include setting organizational objectives, managing budgets, improving work procedures, coordinating interdepartmental work activities, developing teamwork, and making decisions.

A fourth source of information is the identification of exemplary performers who are meeting or exceeding performance criteria. The information gained through interviews can be used to evaluate career pathing and succession planning and to improve the development of the workforce. In an assignment with a major restaurant chain, our interviews focused on three areas: (1) the current position and what skills and experiences prepared employees for success; (2) the challenges of the current position and what knowledge, skills, or experiences would have helped prepare employees; and (3) the impact (if any) that employees feel organizational changes have or will have on the work they do.

Obviously, when you consider implementing a training program, assessment work is mandatory. A great deal of information is required before you can move forward with a performance improvement effort designed for organizational impact. The HR professional plays a key role in contributing to performance effectiveness within the organization.

References and Suggested Readings

Cline, E. B., & Siebert, P. S. (1993). Help for first-time needs assessors. *Training and Development, 47*(5), 99–101.

Dolliver, S. K. (1993). To train or not to train? *Supervision, 54*(10), 12–15.

Edwards, B., Fiore, P., & Van Lare, J. (1994). *Conducting the training needs analysis.* New York: Training By Design.

Filipczak, B. (1994). Needs assessment software. *Training, 31*(12), 69.

Freeman, J. M. (1993). Human resources planning—training needs analysis. *Management Quarterly, 34*(3), 32–34.

Goldstein, I. L. (1993). *Training in organizations: Needs assessment, development, and evaluation* (3rd ed.). Pacific Grove, CA: Brooks/Cole Publishing.

Kaufman, R. (1994). Auditing your needs assessments. *Training and Development, 48*(2), 22–23.

Mager, R. F., & Pipe, P. (1984). *Analyzing performance problems* (2nd ed.). Belmont, CA: Lake Publishing.

McClelland, S. (1992). A systems approach to needs assessment. *Training and Development, 46*(8), 51–53.

McClelland, S. (1994). Training needs assessment data-gathering methods: Part 1, Survey questionnaires. *Journal of European Industrial Training, 18*(1), 22–26.

Nagro, R. G. (1994). Skills assessment takes a high-tech turn. *HRMagazine, 39*(6), 107–111.

Robinson, D. G., & Robinson, J. C. (1995). *Performance consulting.* San Francisco: Berrett-Koehler Publishers.

Rummler, G. A., & Brache, A. P. (1988). The systems view of human performance. *Training Magazine, 25*(9), 45–53.

Schmitt, N. W., & Klimoski, R. J. (1991). *Research methods in human resources management.* Cincinnati, OH: South-Western Publishing.

CHAPTER 9

EVALUATING TEAM PERFORMANCE

James R. Jose

One of the demands imposed by the transformation from high command and control to participative organizational cultures has been the requirement to change the evaluation of work perform-ance. We have been challenged to transition from evaluating peo-ple who perform in their individual capacities to evaluating people who perform as members of groups or teams. Like any dimension of organizational transition, team performance evaluation requires a shift of paradigms from single-rater processes to multi-rater processes and from an individual contributor focus to a more synergistic focus.

However, this shift does not require the abandonment of all of the definitive features of traditional evaluation models. For exam-ple, evaluating the effectiveness of teams requires performance expectations that are linked to business objectives and organiza-tional values. Performance measures are essential, as are clear and easily understood rating systems. Individual development can continue to be at the core of the evaluation effort. Finally, conse-quences in the form of recognition and rewards (or lack thereof for nonachievement) should be an integral part of the evaluation process.

The shift to the evaluation of teams rather than individuals presents both raters and those being rated with special circum-stances and opportunities. Teams are expected to have goals and objectives that they have, in large part, developed themselves. Teams typically are intentionally composed of individuals with diverse backgrounds, experiences, longevity, and levels of influ-ence. This diversity factor heightens the propensity for periodic value conflicts that must be managed by the team. This factor also creates an opportunity for the emergence of multiple and highly diverse options for goal achievement.

A wide range of interpersonal HR knowledge, skills, and abilities must be applied with more intensity in a team-based environment. Team members must make a commitment to learn these skills and to be evaluated on them. For example, some knowledge about personality and decision-making types is desirable, as are highly developed collaborative and cooperative skills. The ability to participate constructively and encourage other team members to do the same is necessary to produce results. This means, at a minimum, that the giving and receiving of constructive feedback must be mastered.

Single- and multi-rater team evaluation processes are used in organizations today. The characteristics of the organizational culture usually determine which process is used. Specifically, the extent to which teams are valued as a way of getting work done, as well as whether or not they are encouraged to mature to a high performing level, is critical. The experience of the organization with the performance evaluation process and how the process is typically implemented in the organization are important determinants as well.

Single-Rater Process Model

The single-rater process would be the preference of organizations that create teams primarily to work ad hoc, finite initiatives, such as division-level reorganizations, designing strategic plans, and developing workplace diversity programs. These organizations typically have not had extensive experience with teamwork. They have performance appraisal processes that are supervisor-driven, sometimes, although usually not, with input from other sources, such as the employees themselves, peers, and clients. The culture is characterized as hierarchical and high command-control, possibly with some tentative experience with teams. Teamwork is typically not highly valued as a way of getting work done.

The individual or group responsible for overseeing the work of the team is the rater, usually referred to as the team sponsor or steering committee. Team members may be asked informally for their perspective on their performance, but this feedback is not normally formalized as a part of the evaluation.

Performance feedback may be provided to the team and to individual team members throughout the life of the team. Periodic progress checks usually take place at key milestones established in the team charter. Formal performance evaluations are completed in accordance with the company's performance appraisal timetable, usually annually.

Multi-Rater Process Model

The multi-rater process would be more appealing to organizations that have had successful experiences with teamwork and have moved beyond the traditional supervisor-driven performance evaluation process. These organizations would have had some experience with the 360-degree feedback process. This process would have achieved a reasonable degree of acceptance within the employee group as a desirable and effective performance evaluation method. The culture is typically in the process of moving from high command-control to being more highly participative in nature, and the number of supervisory levels has been compressed. Teamwork would have a moderate to high level of acceptance as a way of getting work done.

Raters would include the team itself, acting either collectively or individually; the sponsor; the steering committee or team leader to whom the team is responsible; and the representatives of client groups and possibly of other stakeholders, if they exist. The team's self-evaluation and those of all other participants are considered formal parts of the evaluation.

Performance feedback to individuals and to the team as a whole is provided as an integral part of team operation. Team members are comfortable giving and receiving caring, constructive feedback as needed, as requested, or both, especially during team meetings. Formal progress checks take place at key milestones established in the team charter. Formal performance evaluations are completed in accordance with the company's performance appraisal timetable.

In both the single- and multi-rater processes, the team evaluation focuses on the performance expectations and results established in the team charter. The evaluation includes comments that reference

- The impact of team activities on the business objectives and values of the company and any client group(s);

- The achievement of goals (key deliverables) according to pre-established milestones;

- The identification of team behavior trends, such as adhering to operating ground rules; giving and receiving caring, constructive feedback; and providing opportunities for team members to make individual contributions and to participate; and

- The identification of team strengths and growth opportunities for the next performance period.

In conclusion, experience reveals several guidelines that should be observed in the evaluation of team performance. First, the evaluation should be deliberate and have a purpose. Generally, there are three predominant team evaluation purposes, which can be employed individually or in combination. These purposes are as follows:

1. To assess the extent to which the team is producing results and accomplishing its mission and objectives,

2. To determine how well the team is functioning as a participative decision-making organization, and

3. To measure individual team member performance.

Second, team evaluation should have a self-evaluation component. The more mature the team, the greater the chances of the team knowing itself well and being willing to share that knowledge for its own betterment and that of the organization as a whole.

Third, evaluating individual as well as team performance is important. This evaluation is based on the assumption that team members are valued for the special gifts they bring to the mission; and, in turn, the team is valued by how well it elevates and integrates those gifts to produce the intended results.

References and Suggested Readings

Campion, M. A., & Higgs, A. C. (1995). Design work teams to increase productivity and satisfaction. *HRMagazine, 40*(10), 101–107.

Chang, Richard Y. (1994). *Measuring team performance: A practical guide to tracking team success.* Irvine, CA: R. Chang Associates, Publications Division.

Convey, S. (1994). Performance measurement in cross-functional teams. *CMA, The Management Accounting Magazine, 68*(5), 13–15.

Drexler, A., Sibbet, D., & Forrester, R. (1994). *The team performance model, team building: Blueprints for productivity and satisfaction.* Bethel, ME: NTL Institute and University Associates.

Enger, S. M. (1993, Spring). Scorekeeping for world class performance. *The Michigan CPA, 6*–7.

Fisher, R., & Thomas, B. (1996). *Real dream teams: Seven practices used by world class leaders to achieve extraordinary results.* Del Ray Beach, FL: St. Lucie Press.

Hagerman, J. (1995). Teams and measurable results. *CMA, The Management Accounting Magazine, 69*(2), 6.

Harrington-Mackin, D. (1994). *The team building tool kit: Tips, tactics, and rules for effective workplace teams.* New York: AMACOM (American Management Association).

Hoevemeyer, V. A. (1993). How effective is your team? *Training and Development, 47*(9), 67–71.

Jones, S. D., Buerkle, M., Hall, A., Rupp, L., & Matt, G. (1993). Work group performance measurement and feedback: An integrated comprehensive system for a manufacturing department. *Group and Organization Management, 18*(3), 269–291.

Katzenbach, J. R., & Smith, D. K. (1993). The wisdom of teams. Boston: Harvard Business School Press.

Meyer, C. (1994). How the right measures help teams excel. *Harvard Business Review, 73*(3), 95–103.

Parker, G. M. (1994). *Cross functional teams: Working with allies, enemies, and other strangers.* San Francisco: Jossey-Bass.

Scott, D., & Townsend, A. (1994). Teams: Why some succeed and others fail. *HRMagazine, 39*(8), 62–67.

Shonk, J. H. (1992). *Team-based organizations: Developing a successful team environment.* Homewood, IL: Business One Irwin.

Vogt, J. F., & Murrell, K. L. (1990). *Empowerment in organizations: How to spark exceptional performance.* San Diego, CA: Pfeiffer & Company.

Zenger, J. H., Musselwhite, E., Hurson, K., & Perrin, C. (1994). *Leading teams: Mastering the new role.* Homewood, IL: Business One Irwin.

Zigon, J. (1994, June). Making performance appraisal work for teams. *Training, 31*(6), 58–63.

Zigon, J. (1994). Measuring and paying for work-team performance: Perspectives in human resources. *Proceedings of the Society for Human Resource Management, USA, 46,* 225–232.

CHAPTER 10

PARTICIPATION PROGRAMS AND EMPLOYEE HELP PROGRAMS

Maureen J. Fleming

Introduction

Employee participation and employee help programs have become a major area of interest for employers. Anecdotal evidence strongly suggests that both types of program will immediately improve productivity. At the very least employers should be able to expect employee involvement to result in "warm fuzzy" feelings about the organization.

Participation Programs

Regarding the issue of participation, the HR practitioner must begin by identifying the form of participation that is being discussed. Worker participation can take a variety of forms, including but not limited to autonomous work groups, quality circles, participative work design projects, work rescheduling, participation-based compensation (profit sharing, Scanlon Plans, and Gain Sharing), and employee stock ownership plans (Cascio, 1991).

(Keep in mind that the National Labor Relations Board has ruled that employee committees that have any management involvement may be considered illegal labor organizations [Electromation Inc., 309 NLRB No. 163, 12/16/92] and plan accordingly.)

As HR practitioners, we are often called on to measure the effectiveness of a variety of participation programs. There are a number of ways to design this measurement. The key approaches are qualitative and quantitative.

As stated above, there are many forms of worker participation. The key question about a particular form of work participation is always "Did change occur and was it related to the implementation of a participation program?" The most effective design for answering this question involves the use of a measure before implementing a program, followed by measurement after the program has functioned for a time (i.e., pre-test, post-test design).

Quantitative measures are usually job behaviors or performance measures. For example, if worker rescheduling of hours and days of work is the participation method, we could count the number of controllable rejects before and after workers were permitted to self-schedule working hours. Other outcome measures that might be used are such variables as turnover, absenteeism, accident rates, sales performance, and production rates.

Other possible participation programs for workers might be quality circles, participative work redesign, profit sharing, or employee stock ownership plans. The quantitative measures listed above could easily be applied as the outcome measures for any of these participation programs. The variables listed are only suggestions and many other job- or industry-specific outcome measures may be applied.

Qualitative criteria are generally perceptual or attitudinal measures. The most common approach is the written survey questionnaire. A short Likert-style scale that asks questions about satisfaction with, and the importance of, various aspects of the worker participation approach will often be satisfactory. Again, such data may be gathered both before implementing the participation program and again after a period of usage. In many instances, it would be appropriate to use this measure periodically (every 3 or 6 months) to ensure continued satisfaction with the participation project.

Other qualitative approaches include interviews or direct observations of employees. The interview process would be most meaningful if it contained structured and unstructured questions. Thus, the interviewer might use a Likert-style scale asking for employees' numerical ratings of their satisfaction with the program, followed by open-ended questions on what employees liked most and least about the program. The detailed information that can be obtained through this approach can be very beneficial to the implementation process by providing information for fine tuning a process, by preventing terrible mistakes, or by finding serious omissions in the process.

As an extension of the methods described above, we suggest a triangulation approach that allows HR practitioners to increase their confidence in the outcome data that they generate (Zamanou & Glaser, 1994). In a simple pre-test, post-test design, this approach uses three separate techniques to measure change. First, a Likert-style survey questionnaire focusing on attitudes and perceptions about the form of participation should be administered at all levels of the organization. This should be followed by one-on-one structured Likert-style interviews of as many employees as is feasible at a variety of levels in the organization. Finally, the HR researcher should seek critical incidents from all parties.

The data may then be analyzed. The survey questionnaire should yield numerical data that give positive or negative feedback about the efficacy of the participation method. The Likert-style part of the interview data may be analyzed in the same numerical way. Critical incidents from the interview will then cast light on the major and minor benefits and difficulties of the participation system. Figure 10–1 shows the relationships we have described.

It is important to remember that worker participation schemes can often become worker alienation schemes. One must be aware of all the situational factors that may affect the participation process. Lack of involvement of middle management personnel, who in turn refuse to allow "real" participation, results in alienation, but external labor market conditions that increase internal productivity as a result of fear of job loss can strongly affect all outcome measures. It is critically important for the HR practitioner to scan the internal and external environment for factors that might contaminate or interact with the results, thereby presenting a false set of outcomes.

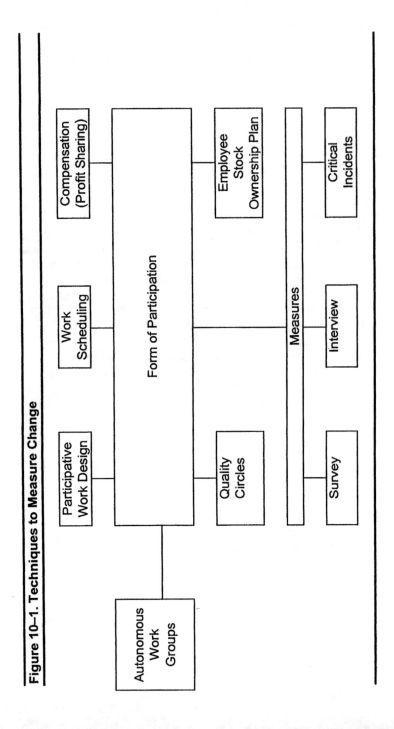

Figure 10–1. Techniques to Measure Change

Employee Assistance Programs

For more than 50 years, companies have offered some form of employee counseling to employees. The early programs focused on drug and alcoholism counseling. Today the range of services is much broader. Marital and family problems, emotional disorders, stress, financial problems, and career counseling are among the many available service areas of Employee Assistance Programs (EAPs). Usually the service is provided by an outside contractor because confidentiality is promised to employees.

Organizations have implemented EAPs for two major reasons: as a rationale for supervisors to confront problem employees and to suggest that they seek assistance, or as a resource for employees to use on a self-initiated basis for themselves or their families. The special feature of the EAP is that a company neither expects nor wants the majority of its employees to use the service. The company, although interested in actual usage by employees, is most concerned that employees be aware of the service and find it to be an attractive employment benefit.

For the HR practitioner, this approach creates a dilemma. To justify the continuation of an EAP program, the company must show that it is used and is perceived as useful, but under no circumstances may it breach the confidentiality promised to users. The best information about actual usage should be obtained from the outside provider. In most instances the outside provider will supply the number of employee visits segmented by category of usage (e.g., alcohol counseling, financial counseling, and so forth).

The internal question of value is best determined by survey data. One of the most important variables to study is employee confidence in the program. Two other issues that should be considered are the importance of the service and general satisfaction with the service.

A simple survey may be constructed that lists the available services and asks raters to indicate their confidence in, their satisfaction with, and the importance of their being offered the service on scales of 1 to 10, with 10 being the highest value. (See Figure 10–2.)

Figure 10–2. Employee Confidence and Satisfaction Survey

Please rate these services on a scale of 1 to 10, with 10 being highest in terms of the importance of offering, confidence in the service, and satisfaction with the service.

EAP Service	Importance of Offering	Confidence in the Service	Satisfaction With the Service
Stress Counseling	——	——	——
Family Counseling	——	——	——
Alcohol and Drug Counseling	——	——	——
Legal Counseling	——	——	——
Career Counseling	——	——	——
Financial Counseling	——	——	——

1

5

10

Strongly disagree

Neutral

Strongly Agree

The data may be analyzed by averaging the responses for each category. After this analysis, it would be appropriate to do some structured interviews to identify the basis of problem areas raised in the survey.

It is important for the HR practitioner to keep in mind that, in the area of EAPs, the company may want to continue to offer the service even if it does not show extensive use. EAPs have become benefits more important in terms of availability than in their usage.

References and Suggested Readings

Cascio, W. F. (1991). *Applied psychology in personnel management.* Englewood Cliffs, NJ: Prentice-Hall.

Marchington, M., Wilkerson, A., Ackers, P., & Goodman, J. (1994). Understanding the meaning of participation: Views from the workplace. *Human Relations, 47*(8), 867.

Milne, S. H., Blum, T. C., & Roman, P. M. (1994). Factors influencing employees' propensity to use an employee assistance program. *Personnel Psychology, 47*(1), 123.

Miner, J. D., & Crane, D. P. (1995). *Human resource management.* New York: Harper Collins.

Pollock, E. J. (1995, November 28). Workers want more money, but they also want to control their own time. *Wall Street Journal,* p. B1.

Schmidt, N. W., & Klimoski, R. J. (1991). *Research methods in human resource management.* Cincinnati, OH: South-Western Publishing.

Wilpert, B. (1995). Organizational behavior. *Annual Review of Psychology, 46,* 59–90.

Zamanou, S., & Glaser, S. R. (1994). Moving toward participation and involvement. *Group and Organization Management, 19*(4), 475–502.

CHAPTER 11

ETHICAL DECISION-MAKING STRATEGIES FOR HUMAN RESOURCE PROFESSIONALS

Carolyn Wiley

Do corporations have an inherent moral obligation or moral responsibility to their employees? This question prevailed throughout the business cycle of the 1980s. The advent of junk bonds, leveraged buyouts, and insider-trading scams and their collective impact on employees and shareholders dominated the business literature of that period. Yet, the very question of whether management ought to engage in moral decision making is, in itself, an ethical dilemma. If managers do not engage in ethical decision making, who will?

Indeed, managers are faced with myriad ethical dilemmas, and they are the ones who are saddled with resolving these dilemmas. As such, they make decisions that have significant effects on the corporation and its human resources. Thus, this chapter focuses on presenting several strategies for ethical decision making. These strategies can be used by general managers, as well as by HR professionals and managers, to enhance their ability to make "good" decisions vis-à-vis ethical dilemmas.

Formal and Informal Strategies

To improve ethical decision making, organizations are adopting strategies characterized as either "formal" or "informal" (Cava, West, & Berman, 1995, p. 29; Wiley, 1995, pp. 24–26). The formal strategies include explicit codes of conduct and related documents. The informal strategies are the implicit guidelines or ethical principles that are best disseminated through training, leadership, and communication.

Formal Strategies. In adopting a formal strategy to improve ethical decision making, an organization may choose to create a *code of ethics* or a *code of conduct*. Such codes establish rules that prescribe acceptable conduct. Moreover, the codes may be considered a formal, written expression of internal or "in-house" law (Cava, West, & Berman, 1995, p. 29), which operates to minimize a company's legal liability to customers or citizens (Ettore, 1992; Laverty, 1989). Organizational codes tend to address common issues, such as respecting proprietary information and avoiding conflicts of interest. To enhance ethical decision making, a code of ethics or standard of conduct should have several attributes. It should provide specific examples, be published, be clear and realistic, be revised periodically, and be enforced (Wiley, 1995, p. 25).

Informal Strategies. Ethical decision making can be improved through informal mechanisms as well. These include maxims or proverbs that reflect an ethical culture (e.g., do unto others as you would have them do unto you). Several questions can be posed to encourage managers to consider many of the hidden facets of difficult organizational issues (Cava, West, & Berman, 1995, p. 29). These include the following:

- Which course of action will do the most good and the least harm?

- What decision can I live with that is consistent with the basic values and commitments in the organization?

- Which alternative best serves others' (stakeholders') rights?

- Which course of action is feasible?

Other informal strategies include training, ethical leadership by example, and regular communication on ethics matters (Cava, West, & Berman, 1995, p. 33). *Training* increases awareness about specific ethical problems that may occur in the workplace and provides employees with appropriate guidance in recognizing and responding to them (Hoffman, 1986).

Ethical leadership creates an ethical climate in which senior management sets the tone of acceptable and expected conduct. Suggestions for improving the ethical climate are (1) identifying the ethical attitudes critical to your company, (2) selecting employees having the desired attitudes, (3) incorporating ethics in the performance evaluation process, (4) establishing a work culture that enforces ethical attitudes, and (5) exhibiting ethical leadership (Goddard, 1988, pp. 43, 45, 47).

Regular communication about ethics aids in explaining the rationale behind leadership policies and actions. Communication takes place in many different settings (such as in staff meetings and newsletters) and through decisions affecting hiring, promotion, and performance appraisals (Cava, West, & Berman, 1995, p. 34).

An Ethical Problem Formulation Model

The problem formulation model (Katsioloudes & Kendree, 1994, p. 83) addresses the process by which organizations collect and interpret data for use in making decisions. This model involves three stages: (1) *recognizing the problem* by noticing conditions that pose organizational threats, (2) *formulating the problem* by interpreting the organizational meaning, and (3) *solving the problem* by making a decision. The process of problem recognition involves the awareness of a discrepancy between the expected and the actual state of affairs.

Once the problem is recognized, the organization must make sense of the information it has gathered. That is, the organization must frame the problem so that it can be solved. Because there are individual and organizational impediments to recognizing ethical problems, explicit organizational structural mechanisms are needed. They include (1) increasing the amount of ethics scanning, (2) establishing explicit ethical standards that can be used to measure for discrepancies, (3) hiring ethicists or providing internal ethics education, and (4) tying project approvals and rewards to ethics compliance. These structural mechanisms ensure that ethical cues are readily noticed and subsequently addressed.

Ethical Decision-Making Behaviors

The variety of unethical behaviors exhibited by managers is almost boundless. Moreover, the potential for individuals and organizations to behave unethically is limitless (Sims, 1992, p. 506). Thus, there is a need to identify some means of improving ethical decision behaviors. Such means include behavioral modeling, managerial controls, corporate ethical modeling, interventions, and organizational development (Knouse & Giacalone, 1992, p. 374). The basic *behavioral modeling* procedure involves viewing videotapes of appropriate and inappropriate behaviors, practicing the behaviors with a trainer (role playing), and receiving taped feedback on the effectiveness of these practiced behaviors. A major advantage of behavioral modeling is that employees can adapt appropriate behaviors to their own styles.

Managerial controls, such as social audits, provide another way of improving ethical decision-making behaviors. Dow Corning's Ethics System shows how audits (Byrne, 1992, p. 69) can uncover major ethics problems (see Figure 11–1).

Figure 11–1. Dow Corning's Ethics System

- Six managers serve 3-year stints on a Business Conduct Committee.

- Two members audit every business operation every 3 years.

- Auditors hold 3-hour reviews with up to 35 employees.

- Auditors report their results to a three-member Audit and Social Responsibility Committee of the board of directors.

Corporate ethical modeling provides guidance on what is appropriate and inappropriate behavior. Moreover, it can provide guidance on translating managerial beliefs into ethical behaviors and on clarifying the organizational instrumentalities between ethical behaviors and rewards or punishments.

Interventions (e.g., grievances, in-house whistle-blowing, suggestion systems, and hotlines) give employees a procedure for internal problem solving.

Organizational development efforts (e.g., workshops, therapy, and leadership influence) can aid in the advancement of better ethical decision making. Workshops or training programs to help employees deal with ethical dilemmas might present a useful seven-step checklist like the one that follows (Schermerhorn, 1989; Otten, 1986):

- Recognize and clarify the dilemma.

- Get all the pertinent facts.

- List all of your options.

- Test each option by asking whether it is legal, right, or beneficial.

- Make your decision.

- Double check your decision by asking yourself how you would feel if your decision was printed in the local newspaper.

- Take action.

A Decision-Making Model Incorporating Ethical Values

The initial influence on decision making comes from the personal values of the decision maker. These personal values provide the underpinning for ethical decisions in private life. However, in professional life, personal values are mediated by other forces inside the organization. These forces (e.g., organizational culture, organizational climate, and organizational and stakeholder goals) alter the role played by personal values in ethical decision making (Fritzsche, 1991, pp. 842–843). Moreover, they influence the recognition and perception of the ethical components of strategic and tactical problems. The set of decision alternatives for these problems also reflects the personal values of the decision maker and the mediating factors. Once the set of decision alternatives has been established, each alternative is evaluated on the basis of criteria (or decision dimensions) related to economic, political, technological, social, and ethical issues. The importance of each criterion varies according to the situation.

The actual decision process may be considered a phased heuristic in which a conjunctive rule specifies a minimum cutoff point for each of the decision dimensions. An ethical conjunctive rule might be "Any alternative that involves a conflict of interest

will be dropped from consideration." Decision alternatives sur-
viving the first phase may then be subjected to another heuristic,
yielding the overall value of each alternative. The attractiveness of
a decision alternative decreases as its potential negative conse-
quences increase. Finally, the selection and implementation of a
decision alternative will have internal and external impacts. Internal impacts affect the organization's climate and goals. External
impacts may alter the set of decision alternatives evoked in the
future.

This model provides a framework in which personal values
are a major input into the decision-making process. The model
offers a means of understanding how organizational forces interact
with the values of individual decision makers to influence the ethical aspects of their decisions. The type of interaction that occurs
depends on the composition and strength of the decision maker's
personal values and on the strength and nature of the organization's mediating factors.

A Framework for Ethical Analysis in Human Resource Management

Ethical analysis starts with a calculation of the content of the dilemma. The content analysis of the dilemma is done within five
classifications (e.g., financial, legal, organizational, social, and
personal) in order to identify all of the benefits and drawbacks
associated with the different courses of action. After the content of
an ethical dilemma has been examined and the financial, legal,
organizational, social, and personal impacts have been identified, a
decision must be made. This decision may be based on subjective
moral standards of behavior or on objective ethical systems of belief (Hosmer, 1987, pp. 316–319). Subjective moral standards include traditions, whereas objective ethical systems of belief
include a rational set of moral standards that recognize the rights
and needs of others.

Normative philosophers have been working since Plato's time
(427 to 347 B.C.) to establish a set of moral standards based on an
essential value that would determine whether an act was "right" or
"wrong." Because ethical choices in management and HR management, in particular, can be seen as compromises among financial,

legal, organizational, social, and personal effects on the company, understanding philosophy or the major ethical systems of belief may help managers to make rational ethical choices (Hosmer, 1987, p. 321; Wiley, 1995, pp. 22–24).

Conclusions

The issue of effectively integrating ethics into business and HR management decisions is a major area of concern for today's corporate leaders. Ethical decisions in business are often difficult to make. Yet, in the pursuit of profits, businesses have a primary need to safeguard the welfare of their employees, community, and other stakeholders. Businesses cannot afford to exploit human resources or to extract natural resources at any cost. Thus, there is the need to improve ethical decision making among business leaders and HR professionals.

A successful method, model, or process for resolving ethical dilemmas should use a practical framework for decision making. This framework should blend the successful experiences of corporations with organizational culture, personal values, and ethical principles. Three such models (frameworks) were presented in this chapter: an ethical problem formulation model, a decision-making model incorporating ethical values, and a framework for ethical analysis in HR management. In addition, theories and the study of ethics and ethical behavior in business can be useful as decision-making tools. In this chapter, for example, ways of improving ethical behaviors, such as behavioral modeling and organizational development, were identified. Ultimately, what is important is that ethical considerations are given priority in strategically managing business operations. The challenge is to select a strategy, model, or process that corresponds with the organization's ethics goals and the individual's personal values and that promotes successful ethical decision-making behaviors among managers.

References and Suggested Readings

Byrne, J. A. (1992, March 9). The best-laid ethics programs. *Business Week, 3*(55), 67–69.

Cava, A., West, J., & Berman, E. (1995). Ethical decision making in business and government: An analysis of formal and informal strategies. *Spectrum: The Journal of State Government,* *68*(2), 28–36.

Colero, L. (1992, March). Ethical approach to business. *Executive Excellence,* *9*(3), 20.

Ettorre, B. (1992). Corporate accountability '90s style: The buck had better stop here. *Management Review,* *81*(4), 16–21.

Fritzsche, D. J. (1991). A model of decision making incorporating ethical values. *Journal of Business Ethics,* *10*(11), 841–852.

Goddard, R. W. (1988). Are you an ethical manager? *Personnel Journal,* *67*(3), 38–47.

Hoffman, W. (1986). What is necessary for corporate moral excellence. *Journal of Business Ethics,* *5*(3), 233–242.

Hosmer, L. T. (1987). Ethical analysis and human resource management. *Human Resource Management,* *26*(3), 313–330.

Katsioloudes, M. I., & Kendree, J. M. (1994). An organizational model of ethical problem recognition and formulation. *Business and Professional Ethics Journal,* *13*(4), 81–93.

Knouse, S. B., & Giacalone, R. A. (1992). Ethical decision making in business: Behavioral issues and concerns. *Journal of Business Ethics,* *11*(5,6), 369–377.

Laverty, E. (1989). The ethical context of administrative decisions: A framework for analysis. *Public Administration Quarterly,* *13*(3), 375–387.

Otten, A. L. (1986, July 14). Ethics on the job: Companies alert employees to potential dilemmas. *Wall Street Journal,* 17.

Schermerhorn, J. R. (1989). *Management for productivity.* New York: John Wiley.

Sims, R. R. (1992). The challenge of ethical behavior in organizations. *Journal of Business Ethics,* *11*(7), 505–513.

Wiley, C. (1995). The ABCs of business ethics: Definitions, philosophies, and implementation. *Industrial Management,* *37*(1), 22–27.

CHAPTER 12

COSTING HR

Eric Anton Kreuter

In examining the design and implementation of effective HR measurement techniques, an HR practitioner must consider certain cost analyses. "Historically, the HR function has defied quantification or measurement, which has left HR professionals ill-prepared to demonstrate that human resources are a form of capital, not solely a line entry of expense: (McDonald & Smith, 1995, p. 59). The authors described a recent study by Hewitt Associates analyzing data from 437 large companies with programs to manage the performance of their people. They found that companies with such programs outperform companies without them. Improvements cited included higher profits, increased stock value, higher sales, and lower growth in numbers of employees (McDonald & Smith, 1995). McDonald and Smith (1995) concluded that "managing human resources provides a payoff in bottom-line financial performance" (p. 59). The study further noted that performance management was key to improving financial results of troubled companies. Therefore, evidence suggests that even for an entity in financial trouble, resources expended to assess performance yield positive financial results.

HR managers need to develop a thorough understanding of business. "The competitive, global environment in which firms operate today requires all managers, including those in HR, to understand and focus upon key business imperatives and concepts" (Berra & Whitford, 1995, p. 83). The main objective of any manager is to maximize shareholder wealth coinciding with corporate strategic planning. Some plans will be oriented toward the short term and others toward long-range goals. "Stock prices and trading volume provide daily evaluation of the firm's management team" (Berra & Whitford, 1995, p. 84).

Performing Costing Analysis

Applying basic cost accounting principles to HR management is necessary and comparatively easy. The first step is a detailed cost-benefit (c/b) analysis. The c/b ratio measures the relative success for a given course of action. It is helpful to view expenses associated with solution endeavors as investments. This approach provides a clearer picture of the return on that investment, or its benefit. The simple approach to cost determination is to prepare a schedule of all actual or possible categories of expenses or benefits. Then the relevant cost in dollars associated with each expense or benefit can be calculated. The following example illustrates the use of this technique:

Problem: Overtime pay is exceeding budget.

Possible solution: Hire additional worker; eliminate overtime.

Step 1: Determine relevant costs associated with possible solution.

Base compensation	$20,000
Fringe benefits @ 25%	5,000
Training costs	2,000
Recruitment costs	3,000
Other costs	1,000
Total relevant costs	$31,000

Step 2: Project benefit.

Reduced overtime hours per annum	1,800
Total overtime cost per hour	$ 19
Total reduced overtime cost per annum	$42,750
(1,800 x $19) × 125%	

Step 3: Calculate savings.

Total reduced overtime costs	$42,750
Total relevant costs	(31,000)
Annual savings	$11,750

Conclusion: Hiring an additional worker and eliminating overtime will generate an annual saving of $11,750. Therefore, the benefit is greater than the cost.

Not all costs and benefits will be easy to measure. Mercer (1989) maintains the following:

> Obviously, some are easier to measure than others. Nonetheless, human resource managers must take it upon themselves to calculate all the possible monies involved in any human resources solutions to business problems. In this way everyone possesses a measure of how effective the human resources endeavors have been (Mercer, 1989, p. 15).

Mercer further recommends conservativism in doing cost accounting. All organized bodies of accounting and management would concur that it is best to present analyses realistically. In performing costing analysis, key ratio types to consider are financial leverage, liquidity, profitability, and asset productivity. They are useful in determining the impact or potential impact of past or future decisions.

Measuring the Economic Impact of Corporate Restructuring

Corporate restructurings have a significant impact on the cost analysis functions of managing human resources. "Although the administration of corporate early-outs is done by human resource managers, few understand the economic rationale behind the apparent obsession that America's CEOs have with restructuring" (Berra & Whitford, 1995, p. 96). An interesting phenomenon is that some stock prices increase substantially following an announcement of a planned restructuring.

If managed properly, a workforce reduction will not result in decreases in revenues. This revenue status is due to expected increases in worker productivity. The savings per worker can be calculated by taking into consideration the workers' base salary and adding fringe benefit costs, then subtracting applicable corporate tax deductions and factoring into the future with an estimated inflation percentage. By decreasing costs, the company will decrease its need for capital. This results in a dramatic impact on the company's cost of operating. Table 12–1 illustrates this concept.

Table 12–1. The Impact of a Workforce Reduction on Profitability

Action: Reduction in Workforce by 5%

Total number of terminated workers: 10
Average base compensation: $35,000
Fringe benefit factor: 25%
Other costs per worker: $3,000
Applicable combined tax rate: 50%
Total savings calculated as follows:

Reduced compensation	$350,000
Reduced fringe benefits	87,500
Reduced other costs	30,000
Total reduced costs	$467,500

Capital costs:

Reduced capital costs @ 8%	37,400
Reduced combined costs	504,900
Less reduced tax benefit	(252,450) *
Net benefit	$252,450

* As a result of reduced cost, tax deductions will also decrease, yielding net savings of $252,450.

Offsetting this savings will be the exit compensation package, usually paid as a lump sum of salary and benefits. The after-tax cost can be calculated, resulting in a current cost matched to the after-tax present value of an early-out restructuring. Therefore, each restructuring can be evaluated on the basis of its projected impact on the net present value (NPV) of the company's equity. The NPV measures the expected change in total stockholder wealth.

Within the costing analysis, HR managers and the corporate officers need to consider the potential negative impact of a restructuring on employee morale. "Thus, the early-out program could potentially decrease revenues or at least slow their growth significantly" (Berra & Whitford, 1995, p. 98). Some restructurings have a negative impact caused by expense reductions resulting in harm to the company's long-term economic viability.

Companies have been spending large sums of money to develop performance appraisal systems, many of which are later abandoned. This is due largely to dissatisfaction with the systems. For example: "Pratt & Whitney (P & W), the jet engine division of United Technologies, made significant changes in its appraisal system in three consecutive years only to abandon the system for a completely different approach the very next year" (Bernadin, Kane, Ross, Spina, & Johnson, 1995, p. 463). Opponents of formal appraisal systems argue that fluctuation in performance is a function of system characteristics rather than individual characteristics. "Reengineering of operational processes to create a customer-focused organization suggests an accompanying reengineering of performance appraisal systems" (Bernadin et al., 1995, p. 464).

For a pay-for-performance compensation system to work effectively, performance measurement is required. The design of an effective appraisal system is a challenge to organizations. "The details of the plan should be reviewed in order to design an appraisal system consistent with the overall goals of the organization and the environment in which the organization exists" (Bernadin et al., 1995, p. 468). In a study by the National Research Council, it was concluded that "The search for a high degree of precision in measurement does not appear to be economically viable in most applied settings; many believe that there is little to be gained from such a level of precision" (Bernadin et al., 1995, pp. 468–469).

Using Automation to Decrease Costs

"The widespread use of desktop personal computers in the workplace has made viable the option of having raters recording performance appraisal ratings directly on computers and using the computer to record performance data" (Bernadin et al., 1995, p. 484). The advantages of this option are lower costs, easy integration of results into the computerized central personnel record systems, and so on. The use of computers eliminates clerical functions, paper records, and files. Such computer use needs to be analyzed in terms of cost, including an assessment of the availability of computer terminals.

Outsourcing

To control varying workloads and to reduce payroll costs, outsourcing has become a popular management tool. According to Syrett (1987):

> The main pressure for innovation in work organisations has derived from employers' efforts to maintain the growth in productivity that they achieved early in the recession by relatively simple means (such as reductions in overmanning and the closure of uneconomic or inefficient plants) and for which the scope is now significantly reduced (Syrett, 1987, p. 121).

In 1994, a survey of 79 companies by the Conference Board indicated that 85% were currently using or planning to use outside firms to handle some of the work of their HR departments. The most frequently outsourced HR functions, according to the survey, were administration of 401(k) plans or other retirement plans, employee assistance programs, wellness or fitness programs, relocation services, and administration of other benefits (The Conference Board, 1994).

As employers look closely at the bottom line contribution of the HR department, those functions that require special expertise or have little "value-added" benefit to the company will continue to be outsourced to specialists and vendors. Outsourcing can benefit a company's HR professionals by freeing them to focus on their most important tasks and by streamlining administrative tasks.

References and Suggested Readings

Bernadin, H. J., Kane, J. S., Ross, S., Spina, J. D., & Johnson, D. L. (1995). Performance appraisal, design, development, and implementation. In G. R. Ferris, S. D. Rosen, & D. T. Barnum (Eds.), *Handbook of human resource management* (pp. 463–489). Cambridge, MA: Blackwell Publishers.

Berra, R. L., & Whitford, D. T. (1995). Analytical financial tools and human resource management. In G. R. Ferris, S. D. Rosen, & D. T. Barnum (Eds.), *Handbook of human resource management* (pp. 83–98). Cambridge, MA: Blackwell Publishers.

The Conference Board. (1994). *HR executive review: Outsourcing HR services*. New York: Author.

McDonald, D., & Smith, A. (1995). A proven connection: Performance management, compensation and business results. In E. L. Gubman (Ed.), *Compensation and benefits review* (p. 59). New York: AMACOM (American Management Association).

Mercer, M. (1989). *Turning your human resources department into a profit center*. New York: AMACOM (American Management Association).

Syrett, M. (1987). New patterns of work. In S. Harper (Ed.), *Personnel management handbook* (pp. 121–135). London: Gower Publishing.

CHAPTER 13

MEASURING ADDED VALUE AND EFFECTIVENESS

H. W. Hennessey, Jr.

This chapter poses some interesting questions. How can it be determined if human resource management (HRM) is adding value to organizations and contributing to organizational effectiveness? Each of these topics would require several books to discuss fully, but few if any comprehensive treatments seem to exist. Therefore, this chapter will try to define some terms and then propose some refinements to the basic questions that may help people in organizations deal with these important, but poorly understood, questions.

Value Added

Traditionally, economists have defined *value added* as the increment to profit in a product that results from a transformational activity. One recent reference (Yeung, Brockbank, & Ulrich, 1994) proposes that the following three issues have driven firms in their efforts to add value through HRM: cost reduction, customer satisfaction, and the push to meet strategic business needs.

Cost reductions can easily be seen as having a clear influence on profit. They have the additional benefit of being relatively easy to measure. HRM has typically lowered costs by increasing the sharing of services across organizational units, by more effectively using information systems, and by outsourcing standardized services. Each of these methods can provide quantifiable cost reductions and direct evidence of the value added by HRM.

Customer satisfaction is influenced indirectly, yet primarily by facilitating the technical performance of HR functions. A major concern as businesses attempt to improve customer satisfaction by shortening cycle times is the need to flexibly redeploy employees in response to changing customer needs. Reengineering of HR's functional responsibilities to expedite routine functions is a contributing factor. Furthermore, line managers are increasingly being reinvolved in HR management as part of this effort. HR's role is shifting back to consultant-expert in cooperation with line management. Information systems that support this decentralization have had a major impact. Measurement of cycle times in HR functional areas holds promise as an indicator of the effectiveness of changes.

Self-managed work teams are finding increasing use as firms attempt to implement quality improvement programs. HR has a significant role in facilitating the development of these teams. Substantial amounts of training are typically required in basic areas like communication and sharing of information, problem solving, and conflict resolution, as is enhanced technical training to facilitate flexibility in team roles. Consequently, HR departments have a major role in the empowerment of teams because of the training they can provide. The resulting changes in group productivity provide indirect evidence of the efficacy of HR interventions. Direct measurement is harder to envision, although the effectiveness of various training interventions could be assessed through observation of team behavior.

Meeting strategic business needs has been the focus of many discussions, centering on the need for HR managers to become full strategic partners in the management of their businesses.

Fulmer (1990) provides some interesting insights into the typical patterns of development of HR's strategic involvement by describing the four stages it moves through.

At Stage 1, HRM programs are typically negative and defensive in outlook. Their main focus is the avoidance of problems—high turnover, unions, and so on.

At Stage 2, HRM organizations are more positive in tone and seem characterized by a desire to "do what is right." HR managers in Stage 2 organizations typically see themselves as professionals and guide their decisions more through loyalty to the profession than to a single employer. These decision-making practices lead to policies and programs that are driven more by personal feelings of what is right than by business objectives.

At Stage 3, top management of firms exhibits high regard for top HR officials, and may include them in some strategic planning sessions. However, HR officials are still viewed primarily as resources, and their involvement in planning is frequently an afterthought. Programs are still justified largely on the basis of cost savings.

At Stage 4, HRM would be seen as a major source of competitive advantage in the marketplace. HR would be treated on an equal level with marketing, finance, and operations. HR staff would be involved from the outset in all planning and would play key roles in designing the methods by which strategies are implemented. The view of HR managers taken by other managers would be that they were management generalists who just happened to have responsibility for HR.

Movement into Fulmer's Stages 3 and 4 provides the most powerful means for HRM to add value to organizations. By early and pervasive involvement, HRM can ensure that the maximum potential is derived from HR within a given strategy. Evaluation of the value added by HRM then becomes an integral part of the evaluation of the entire strategy.

Organizational Effectiveness

From a researcher's perspective, even defining *organizational effectiveness* reminds one of the tar baby of Joel Chandler Harris' *Uncle Remus*. Every time you try to let go to take a fresh grip on the problem, you find that you cannot. The simple definitions that promise easy measurement usually yield incomplete information or limit the ability of the researcher to make comparisons across organizations. The richer, complex, and longitudinal definitions that approximate the real dimensions of effectiveness are difficult to use in actual measurement and yield results that can be difficult to interpret and to understand.

Simple definitions of organizational effectiveness center on meeting the organization's goals. Problems with this approach include the inability of organizations to specify and prioritize their goals and to express the goals in measurable terms. If these problems can be solved, simple models of effectiveness can be useful in tracking one organization's performance over time. Complex definitions of effectiveness may depend on long-term measures of the performance of organizations. Long-term indicators may be unsatisfactory for short-term diagnosis of organizational performance, which is frequently desired by practitioners.

Even if simple models of effectiveness are used, if an organization wishes to assess its effectiveness relative to another organization, it must assume that the goals of other organizations are similar to its own. Some authorities (Pfeffer, 1977) have argued that comparative analysis of effectiveness is the only meaningful measure. Certainly, this is what benchmarking and other attempts to make cross-organizational comparisons have reinforced. A caution, then, is to be as sure as possible of the similarity of the goals of your organization to those of any firm with which you compare yourself. This caution is especially true if these comparisons are intended to gauge the effectiveness of your organization overall in comparison to others.

Benchmarking and Organizational Effectiveness

Benchmarking has become one of the hot topics of HR in recent years. Growing out of the general "quality" movement, benchmarking is sometimes defined as "the process of identifying and learning from best practices anywhere in the world" (Benchmarking Exchange Home Page, 1996). Benchmarking attempts to drive organizations to the realization that they can learn from the experiences of others and avoid costly mistakes in the process. HR is frequently cited as the business process most often targeted for benchmarking. This description should not be surprising given the HR profession's long-term reliance on wage and salary surveys as comparative indicators of pay equity. Benchmarking should be second nature to HR professionals, even though they may not have called it that.

Benchmarking as a practice can add value to an organization just through forcing the careful analysis and consideration of the organization's current processes and goals. Simply increasing understanding and awareness of what is actually going on within the organization can identify many opportunities for cost savings, help eliminate bottlenecks, and rationalize work roles. Comparison with other organizations, the "identified" focus of benchmarking, can offer many new insights and alternatives. However, often the major benefit is from the increased understanding of the organization's own activities.

There is not enough space here for an exhaustive discussion of benchmarking as it is currently discussed in the general management literature. Ideas and practices change constantly. The Internet provides a good avenue for reaching the most current information; one of the best sites is http://www.benchnet.com for the *Benchmarking Exchange Home Page.*

It may be enough to note that our economy's needed emphasis on increased organizational productivity and effectiveness in the age of the service organization necessitates the careful consideration of the effectiveness with which the organization's human resources are employed. People are the major determining factor in the success or failure of service organizations and that will be true for the future that any of us is likely to see. Adding value to organizations is going to occur mainly through enhancement of the human resource.

References and Suggested Readings

Benchmarking Exchange Home Page [Online]. (1996). Use *http://www.benchnet.com* as the URL.

Fulmer, W. (1990). Human resource management: The right hand of strategy implementation. *Human Resource Planning, 13*(1), 1–11.

Pfeffer, J. (1977). Usefulness of the concept. In P. S. Goodman, J. M. Pennings, & Associates (Eds.), *New perspectives on organizational effectiveness* (pp. 132–145). San Francisco: Jossey-Bass.

Yeung, A., Brockbank, W., & Ulrich, D. (1994). Lower cost, higher value: Human resources function in transition. *Human Resource Planning, 17*(3), 1–16.

GLOSSARY

HUMAN RESOURCE HANDBOOK

The following terms are defined as they are used in the context of the chapters in which they appear.

360-Degree Feedback: A multi-rater appraisal system in which supervisors, peers, subordinates, customers, clients, and employees themselves are the raters.

Analytical Survey: Uses the data collected in a polling survey for statistical analysis.

Aptitude Test: The measurement of general ability to learn or acquire a skill.

Assessment Centers: For the observation of job candidates in simulated work situations.

Autonomous Work Groups (also Self-Managing Teams): Work teams that have the authority to manage their own task and interpersonal processes as they carry out their work.

Avoidable Separations: Represents the portion of employee turnover that management has the most opportunity to control.

Behavioral Modeling: Involves viewing videotapes of appropriate and inappropriate behaviors, practicing the behaviors with a trainer (role playing), and receiving taped feedback on the effectiveness of the practiced behaviors.

Behaviorally Anchored Rating Skills: A behavioral approach to performance appraisal that consists of a series of vertical scales, one for each important dimension of job performance.

Benchmark Jobs: Jobs that anchor salary data to the relevant market to have comparability among similar jobs in different parts of organizations.

Benchmarking: Sometimes defined as "the process of identifying and learning from best practices anywhere in the world" (Benchmarking Exchange, Online).

Central Tendency: The measurement of mean, median, or mode in a sample.

Central Tendency Error: An error that occurs when a rater tends to put all ratees toward the middle of the rating scale.

Code of Ethics or Code of Conduct: Establishes rules that prescribe acceptable conduct and may be considered a formal, written expression of internal or in-house law.

Community Office System: A system in which employees from several companies share basic office facilities and related support systems.

Constructive Feedback: The process of individuals sharing data about past performance in a developmental manner to reinforce desirable behaviors or change undesirable behaviors (constructive feedback is an essential characteristic of effective teamwork).

Content Validity: A validation strategy, relying on the judgment of experts, that is used to determine whether a measure assesses an entire content area.

Control Group: A group that is not exposed to any kind of treatment in an experimental design.

Corporate Ethical Modeling: Provides guidance on what is appropriate and inappropriate behavior; can provide guidance on translating managerial beliefs into ethical behaviors and on clarifying the organizational instrumentalities between the ethical behaviors and the rewards or punishments.

Cost-Benefit Analysis: A technique used to compare total resources required with total benefits from each program, system, service, unit, or activity.

Critical Incident Method: A method of identifying job tasks that are important for job success.

Employee Stock Ownership Plan: A philosophical belief in employee ownership; also may be an inexpensive way to borrow money, or an additional employee benefit.

Experimental Group: A group that receives some kind of treatment (or change in working conditions) in an experimental design.

External Equity: Demonstrates how employees can compare their pay rates with the rates of similar positions that are in other organizations.

Forced Choice Method: An approach to performance appraisal that requires the rater to choose from statements designed to distinguish between successful and unsuccessful performance.

Functional Job Analysis: A job analysis procedure, developed by the U.S. Department of Labor, that provides standardization for rating and comparing different jobs (it concentrates on the work performed and on worker traits).

Gain Sharing: A philosophy of cooperation in which an involvement system is tied to a financial bonus.

Graphic Rating Scale Method: A trait approach to performance appraisal where each employee is rated according to a scale of characteristics.

Graphonalysis: Analysis of handwriting to identify personality characteristics.

Halo Effect: A rating error in which the rater's overall impression of the ratee is based on one dimension of that ratee and not total dimensions of performance.

Impairment Testing: A test to detect actual impairment of motor skills and hand-eye coordination.

In-Basket Exercise: A behavioral test designed to evaluate certain skills in a controlled environment (usually during assessment activities).

Informed and Voluntary Consent: Requires researchers to apprise potential participants about a study before the participants become involved in it (participants should be advised that they have the right to withdraw their consent at any time during the research process).

Internal Equity: Demonstrates how employees view their pay in relation to others within the organization.

Involuntary Turnover: Occurs when an employee is discharged or terminated, often for just cause.

Job Analysis: A systematic examination of the knowledge, skills, and abilities (KSAs) required for the performance of the duties and responsibilities of a job.

KSAs: The knowledge, skills, and abilities of job applicants.

Leniency or Strictness Error: A performance rating error in which the appraiser tends to give a group of employees either unusually high or unusually low ratings.

Likert Scale: Grades responses to questions or statements in terms of five categories: strongly agree (SA), agree (A), undecided (U), disagree (D), and strongly disagree (SD).

Multi-Rater Assessment: See 360-Degree Feedback.

Net Present Value (NPV): Measures the expected change in total stockholder wealth.

Networking: A system in which a parent company selects and trains volunteers to leave the parent company and establish their own businesses based at home, in community offices, or in independent locations (company offshoots are connected to the parent company via computer).

Organizational Culture: The shared philosophies, values, beliefs, norms, and altitudes that knit an organization together.

Performance Appraisal: The process of identifying, observing, measuring, and developing human performance in organizations.

Performance Measures: Quantifiable core indicators of the effectiveness of an organizational unit or individual.

Polling Survey: A survey that is used to examine current practices and techniques.

Position Analysis Questionnaire (PAQ): A structured questionnaire, consisting of 194 items, that quantitatively samples worker-oriented job elements (job elements include information input, mental processes, work output, relationships with other persons, job context, and other job characteristics).

Power Test: Measurement without time limits of a person's expertise in a subject area.

Preemployment Test: A devise used to assess through paper-and-pencil responses or simulated exercises a candidate's ability to perform a certain job.

Primacy and Recency Errors: The results of heavily weighted incidents or information that either occur early in the review period or are very recent experiences.

Primary Research: Studies performed directly by the researcher using a variety of methodologies.

Profit Sharing: A bonus to employees using some percentage of the company's profits beyond some minimum level.

Protected Group: People who are covered by civil rights and equal employment opportunity legislation for employment opportunities (such groups include women, ethnic minorities, those with disabilities, and those of certain ages).

Quality Circles: Small groups of volunteers who meet regularly to identify, analyze, and solve quality and other related problems pertaining to their work.

Relevant Labor Market: Geographic area or areas where an organization would expect to recruit all potential employees for a job.

Reliability: The degree to which an evaluation technique consistently measures what it purports to measure.

Right to Privacy and Confidentiality: "The right of the individual to decide the extent to which attitudes, opinions, behaviors, and personal facts will be shared with others" (Stone, 1978, p. 147).

Scanlon Plan: See Gain Sharing.

Secondary Research: Studies conducted by persons other than the person who is reporting the research information.

Selection Process: Identifies and matches job applicant qualifications to position requirements in order to choose the most competent candidate.

Selection Ratio: The proportion of candidates who are hired to the number of candidates in the available applicant pool.

Speeded Test: A test that measures processing speed for an activity.

Stakeholder: Any individual or group that has an interest in or is affected by the products and services delivered by the team being evaluated.

Survivor/Wastage Rate: The proportion of new employees who stay with or leave an organization during a specific time period.

Synergistic Organization: An organizational unit that has a highly integrated team whose functioning produces results greater than the sum of the results that could be produced by individuals functioning alone.

Task Analysis: A process undertaken to determine the knowledge, skills, and abilities (KSAs) necessary to complete the various tasks involved in a total job.

Turnover for Avoidable Separation: Represents the portion of employee turnover that management has the most opportunity to control.

Turnover Rate: The number of employee separations during a month divided by the total number of employees at mid-month, expressed as a percentage.

Unavoidable Separations: Represents that portion of employee turnover over which the organization normally has no control.

Validity: The degree to which an evaluation technique truly measures what it is supposed to measure.

Value Added: The increment to profit in a product that results from a transformational activity.

Voluntary Turnover: Occurs when an employee leaves by the employee's own choice.

Work Sample Test: A test that requires the applicant to perform tasks that are actually part of the work required on the job.

INDEX

Page numbers in bold type indicate tables or figures.

ABOUT THE SHRM FOUNDATION

The SHRM Foundation is a nonprofit organization established in 1966 to fund and support applied research, publications, scholarships and educational programs to help HR professionals and their employers prepare for the future. The Foundation's goal is to continuously improve standards of practice and performance for the HR profession and to help HR leaders stay current with the latest developments and trends.

About SHRM

The Society for Human Resource Management (SHRM), the leading voice of the human resource profession, represents the interests of more than 70,000 professional and student members from around the world. SHRM provides its membership with education and information services, conferences and seminars, government and media representation, and publications that equip human resource professionals for their roles as leaders and decision makers within their organizations. The Society is a founding member and Secretariat of the World Federation of Personnel Management Associations (WFPMA), which links human resource associations in 55 nations.

To order additional copies of this book,
please call (800) 444-5006.